Praise for
Inspiring Creativity Through Magick

"A wonderful guide to bringing forth and inspiring your inner muse. Astrea details how to create a magickally productive, creative space and how to use your inner magick in a beautiful, inspiring way. The easy-to-follow advice and rituals included will catapult your artistic side and you will create magick in no time."

—Jen Sankey, author of *Magickal Manifesting with the Moon* and *Stardust Wanderer Tarot*

"Creativity and art are cherished by so many of us, yet it's also common to experience doubt, insecurity, and blocks in the creative process. In *Inspiring Creativity Through Magick*, Astrea Taylor explores the topic of creativity from a variety of magickal and practical angles, providing readers with the tools to not only complete meaningful creative projects, but also keep the fires of inspiration lit. This is a must-read for magick folk who participate in the arts or want to!"

—Durgadas Allon Duriel, author of *Worthy as You Are* and *The Little Work*

"Astrea's words weave a potent mix of practicality and inspiration that will unblock your creative process and unleash the magick within you."

—Hana the Suburban Witch, host of the *Witch Talks* podcast

"With rituals and exercises throughout, this is a true work of art that all practitioners of any craft would benefit from exploring."

—Vincent Higginbotham, author of *How Witchcraft Saved My Life* and *Thrifty Witchery*

"In *Inspiring Creativity Through Magick*, Astrea Taylor displays a deep working knowledge of metaphysical guides and the spirits of creativity. It's a wonderful exploration of inspiration and divine assistance within the creative act and a goldmine for breaking through creative blocks!"

—Laova and Eric Lingen, hosts of
The Spirit World Center podcast

"Astrea Taylor is a gifted storyteller and teacher. In *Inspiring Creativity Through Magick*, she seamlessly blends myth, history, and wisdom with the encouragement for creative practitioners to find their own way. This book is a must-read for those longing to embrace their own creativity, birth a new project, or embrace the spirit of creativity in their daily lives."

—Mandi Em, author of *Happy Witch*
and *Witchcraft Therapy*

"Astrea Taylor has written a book that seamlessly weaves creativity and magick together, revealing in new and exciting ways how one influences the other and how they are inextricably entwined. Crafty witches, magical manifestors, and magicians of all kinds will fall in love with this affirming and useful book that will teach you how to invite spirits of creativity, invoke states of flow, and bless your works so that they transform, heal, delight, and inspire. If you've ever set a pen to paper, written a song, danced, painted, dressed-up, performed, or come up with an inventive solution to a problem, open this book and discover how to enrich your art with magic."

—Madame Pamita, author of *Baba Yaga's Book of Witchcraft*,
The Book of Candle Magic, and *Madame Pamita's Magical Tarot*

INSPIRING

creativity

THROUGH

MAGICK

© Cody Rowlands

About the Author

Astrea Taylor is an eclectic/intuitive pagan witch whose life goals include empowering other witches and encouraging them to use intuition in their witchcraft. She's the author of *Intuitive Witchcraft*, *Air Magic* (the winner of a gold COVR award in 2022), and *Modern Witchcraft with the Greek Gods*. She mentors and presents workshops and rituals online and at festivals across the country. Astrea has contributed passages to several books and magazines, including *Green Egg, We'Moon, Mastering Magick, Llewellyn's Magical Almanac, Llewellyn's Spell-A-Day Almanac, The Witch's Altar, The Witch's Book of Spellcraft, Witchology*, and *Llewellyn's Witches' Companion*. She blogs on Patheos Pagan as Starlight Witch, and she fire dances with Aurora Fire Dancers. Learn more at AstreaTaylor.com.

ASTREA TAYLOR

INSPIRING

creativity

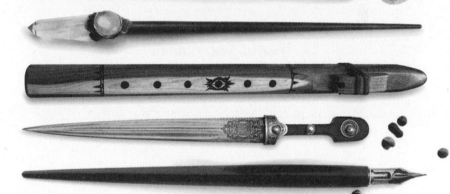

THROUGH

MAGICK

HOW TO RITUALIZE YOUR ART & ATTRACT THE CREATIVE SPIRIT

LLEWELLYN PUBLICATIONS • WOODBURY, MINNESOTA

FIRST EDITION
First Printing, 2023

Cover design by Cassie Willett
Interior art by the Llewellyn Art Department

Llewellyn Publications is a registered trademark of Llewellyn Worldwide Ltd.

Library of Congress Cataloging-in-Publication Data (Pending)
ISBN: 978-0-7387-7015-4

Llewellyn Worldwide Ltd. does not participate in, endorse, or have any authority or responsibility concerning private business transactions between our authors and the public.

All mail addressed to the author is forwarded but the publisher cannot, unless specifically instructed by the author, give out an address or phone number.

Any internet references contained in this work are current at publication time, but the publisher cannot guarantee that a specific location will continue to be maintained. Please refer to the publisher's website for links to authors' websites and other sources.

Llewellyn Publications
A Division of Llewellyn Worldwide Ltd.
2143 Wooddale Drive
Woodbury, MN 55125-2989
www.llewellyn.com

Printed in the United States of America

for Scarlett, who brings the fire,
&
for Crowe, my beloved creative spirit

Disclaimers and Best Practices

The advice in this book is intended to educate and assist people on their quest to become better artists. The magickal practices in this book don't exist in a vacuum and they don't guarantee success—they rely upon artists showing up, doing the work, and learning their craft. Please always ensure your personal safety. Fire safety is important—be cautious of where you place flames, and never leave a lit candle unattended. Be cautious when using oils and herbs in case an allergic reaction could occur. Research herbs and oils to find whether a contraindication exists with your medicine. Don't ingest essential oils, and don't use undiluted essential oils on your skin. Keep essential oils, incense, herbs, smoke, and all other potentially toxic materials away from children and pets. Consult a doctor, therapist, or another health care provider before ingesting herbs and if you have any concerns about your general health or mental health.

Contents

Foreword by Michael Herkes … xiii

Introduction: The Artist as a Magician … 1

PART ONE: THE CREATIVE SPIRIT AND THE CREATIVE RITUAL: CRAFTING YOUR ROUGH DRAFT

Chapter 1: Creative Spirits: Inspiring Art … 15

Chapter 2: Air: Vision and Inspiration … 53

Chapter 3: Fire: Passion and Courage … 73

Chapter 4: Water: Balance and Flow … 95

Chapter 5: Earth: Growth and Perseverance … 111

Chapter 6: Casting the Circle:
Finishing Your Rough Draft … 129

PART TWO: REFINING AND RELEASING YOUR ART INTO THE WORLD

Chapter 7: The Spirit of Your Creation:
Awakening the Egregore … 157

Chapter 8: Creative Alchemy:
Refining Your Art … 169

Chapter 9: The Magician's Reveal:
Releasing Your Art into the World … 181

Chapter 10: Post-Release:
Liminal Rest, Recharge, and Reflection … 199

Conclusion: Art Life … 213

Acknowledgments … 215

Appendix: Deities Associated with Art and Creativity … 217

Bibliography … 221

Foreword

Creativity is to the artist what magick is to the witch—an energy that can be manipulated to create change in the world. Witchcraft is about using your will to create this change. While magic is the manifestation of your intentions, creativity is the conduit to setting your witch work into motion. Both simultaneously help awaken imagination and a sense of wonderment in life.

Magic in and of itself is a creative process. It, along with creativity, allows you the chance to see things in life differently. It all begins with the creation of an intention that uses energetic sources to result in a transformative gain. It is also the selection and arrangement of your tools and ingredients. It is the excitement that ripples through you as you light your candles and hold your crystals. It is the ecstasy stimulated by your actions as you raise the energy within the ritual of a spell. It is walking between the worlds and calling forth your intuitive powers through the senses, seeing the synchronicity and symbols as they unfold in your mind's eye alongside the elements of nature that envelope your physical world.

When you still your mind and pay attention closely, you can experience a symphony of muses as they conduct your primal soul to bestow beauty in the world around you. It is the breath that fills your lungs and the breeze on which birds soar. It is the molten core of our planet, the warmth of the sun in the sky, and the pounding rhythm of your heartbeat. It is the surge of the sea and rivers of water that parallel the blood flowing through your veins. It is the rocks, trees, and mountains that give form and structure like your flesh and bones. It is the spirit within that connects to divinity and the higher self. The witch is an artist and a vessel for creativity to move through.

Being creative is one of the most exciting experiences I have ever felt in this world. I claimed the title of *artist* many years ago—well before that of *witch*. Early in my life, my mother passed down to me the importance of expressing myself creatively. I was encouraged to draw as often as possible, and as I practiced my artistic skills, they evolved from two-dimensional scribbles to forms that mirrored my imaginative urges. Finding new ways to create was also fuel to my inner fire. I learned to master various media, like crayon, colored pencil, marker, charcoal, paint, and photography. This further evolved into fashion and the creative surge to use aesthetic and adornment as visual, living works of art.

At the same time, I was also coming into my magic as a teen witch—seeking out spiritual expression to help find empowerment during my coming of age. As I advanced in my magical studies, I began to feel my worlds of artist and witch intersect. I started to see how my creativity invigorated my magic and vice versa. As I read books on witchcraft and began practicing, I became aware of new creative potentials, gaining intrigue with the beauty of words themselves and how they could be strung together in a way to further extend my artistic expression. Now, having authored a number of books while cultivating my persona as "the Glam Witch," known for centering my practice around the visual art of glamour magic, I have begun using creativity to inspire inner and outer transformation in myself and others.

I absolutely love this book and Astrea's many words of wisdom. I wish I had this resource earlier on in my journey to help focus and align my creative energy with magic in the sophisticated fashion that she has provided. Astrea has created such a wonderful source of ways to magically fuel your creativity and use it to your advantage in creating a life of authentic magical expression to experience and create true transformation in the world.

I am confident that this book will help you conjure the muse within to release imaginative beauty into the world. There are so many spells, rituals, and mythologies included that are integrated in real-life artistic experience that any artist, regardless of their preferred medium, can find useful bites of information they can turn into positive action. Whether you seek inspiration from spirits and elemental energies to spark the fire within, templates to ritualize your creative process, or empathetic encouragement to navigate the peaks and valleys of post-release criticism, Astrea's insight will help you set your creative spirit aflame.

Witchcraft allows you the creative freedom to decorate your life as you see fit. What I've learned over the years as a creative is that honoring my individuality and identity in this world provides me with a stronger way to express myself imaginatively. So tap into your uniqueness. Give yourself the freedom to be the magician who holds a paintbrush as a wand. Continue forth on your creative journey with the pages ahead, and paint the world with your vivid, magical splendor. There is limitless power in this book for forging your creative prowess and embodying your art of witchery. Your time is now.

—Michael Herkes, author of *The GLAM Witch*

The Artist as a Magician

In the winter of 2009, I was deeply engrossed in writing what would become my first finished book when I noticed there was a spirit in the room with me. He showed up at the edge of my vision as a small, shadowy figure who was barely discernible but definitely there. The spirit was no larger than my cat, and he stared at me in a similar manner. Of course, this spirit wasn't my cat. Casper lay curled up beside me on an ottoman whenever I wrote. He was blissfully unaware of the spirit, just as he ignored the items that seemed to give me so much inspiration—my steaming cup of tea, the sodalite I kept beside my laptop, the blue pillar candle that lit up the room, and the rose incense.

I was surprised to see an unfamiliar spirit in my writing room, but not as surprised as other people might be. As a witch, I'd seen many kinds of spirits—I'd even worked magick with them in rituals and spells. However, this spirit was unlike all the other ones I'd seen. I'd never seen one so short and squat. Also, he had somehow gotten through all the protection magick I had woven around my house to keep out random spirits. Even though he was technically an intruder, he didn't act like the other spirits who had trespassed into my home before. There were no whispered lies and no favors asked. There was no negative energy, and he wasn't drawing my energy away from me. It seemed that this polite little spirit didn't want anything from me at all. He was peaceful, patient, and content to stand at the edge of my sight and within my energetic bubble. I felt as if he were waiting for something to happen. All these feelings, as well as my curiosity about what kind of spirit he may be, kept me from banishing him.

That first time I noticed him, I turned so I could get a better look at him. In the brief time it took for my eyes to alight upon the place where he had been, he had vanished. There was nothing there apart from the shiny black wooden floor. There wasn't even a trace of energy to show that he had been there at all. I recall feeling puzzled and somewhat relieved that he was gone even though he didn't seem threatening. However, I didn't linger on it. I didn't need a mystery to solve—I needed to keep writing.

Several days later, when I was writing a very emotional part of my book with the same candle, tea, incense, and sodalite, he appeared again. I instinctively glanced in his direction, but he was gone instantly for the second time. At that point, I stopped writing for a moment to think about the patterns of when he appeared. I realized that the spirit only showed up when I was so entrenched in writing my story that I felt as if I were in another world. When I stopped writing, he didn't seem to exist anymore, at least not in my immediate presence. He also came when I had the exact same items—the tea, the candle, the incense, and the sodalite.

With this knowledge, I formulated a plan to learn more about him. I resolved that I would again use what I began calling my *creative correspondences*. I'd remain focused on my work so I wouldn't scare him away. When he appeared, I'd observe him from the periphery of my sight and try to figure out what kind of spirit he was and what he wanted.

Not long afterward, while I was writing with my creative correspondences, he arrived again. I continued writing while viewing him in more detail. He didn't reveal much of himself, but his shadowy presence took more of a shape. He appeared as a large, black bird, but with some human traits too. To my surprise, he also wore a tiny black suit, a pocket watch, and a monocle, like a gentleman crow from another era. I set my disbelief aside to pay attention to my writing, which started to flow more effortlessly than it had before he arrived. It had been a difficult scene to write, and I was struggling to make my vision of the events intelligible. However, as soon as he arrived, the words came through so much more easily. A pleasurable sensation trickled down from the top of my head, like cool water or an icy breeze that relaxed and invigorated me.

The experience lasted only a few minutes, but I knew it was something magickal. It had the same taste and thrilling feeling as magick, and I was left feeling more amped to be alive.

In the following weeks, whenever he showed up, I kept my eyes focused on my writing, but I welcomed him with a smile. My writing flowed nearly effortlessly. The spirit came more and more often, and I came back to my writing desk more often as well. His arrival had no fanfare; rather, it was marked by his barely discernible appearance and a flow of inspiration. Whenever I wrote something particularly brilliant, he was there, his icy touch sending chills through the top of my head. As a beginning writer, I was shocked at the good quality of my work. Bragging has never been one of my strong suits, but with him around, I couldn't deny that I had an absolutely perfect plot twist, and I couldn't improve the words I'd hastily typed either. Not only was the quality of my writing better, but the quantity was too. I was able to write for longer stretches of time. Our energy together was electric, and I found myself wanting to create more and more.

I decided this spirit was a creative spirit for several reasons. First of all, he didn't care about anything except for my writing. Second, he didn't accept any of the offerings I gave him unless they involved the creative process. He had shrugged at all the drinks and food I left out, even when I tried variations. However, when I created a collage portrait of him, he appreciated it so much that he sent me more creative energy than ever before.

There were several signs that he was a beneficial spirit. After our sessions, I felt energized and elated. I didn't experience any negative side effects from spending time with him, such as an energy drain or a hangover feeling. Sure, I had slight mental strains from time to time, but that could happen to anyone who focused on a creative project for several hours.

The last reason I believed him to be a creative spirit was that he helped me finish my first book ever. Despite having tried to write books for several years, this time was different—he was there.

Since those early years with Crowe, I've worked with him magickally and in many disciplines of art. I've gained insights into the creative process that may not have come had I not cultivated that time with him and appeased him with those creative correspondences.

Since then, I've realized that all magick can be viewed as an art and all art as magick. The two are similar in so many ways. Both artists and magicians create something from nothing. They find the right words, the right materials, and the right way to use them to produce what they desire. They study what's known and experiment with possibilities to find the best fit for their visions. They experience otherworldly states and commune with spirits. Artists create a final product that is much greater than the sum of its parts.

The connection between art and magick has been known for millennia, and it's clear in several phrases and meanings in our language. The word *craft* is synonymous with one's art and a magickal practice. The word *charm* means either a crafted item or a magickal working. *Enchantment* and *incantation* mean singing and casting a spell or some other magickal act. The word *inspired* has magickal, spiritual, and artistic meanings, and it generally means an elevated state of being. Even the word *art* has been used for both creative and magickal endeavors.

To a certain degree, whenever we engage with any kind of art that moves us, we fall under its spell. We encounter a magickal world that someone else has created, and we experience sights, sounds, and feelings conjured by the artist. This is utterly magickal! If you ever experienced this with someone else's art, your creative receptors are open and it's possible that you can create the kind of art that moves other people.

I wrote this book to encourage you to make the art you've been dreaming about. If you're on the fence about whether you should take up writing, singing, dancing, acting, music, drag artistry, or whatever you love, why not try? There are countless benefits to being creative. Art encourages us to be authentic, which helps us better know who we are. With it, we can show other people how we feel. This lets us feel that we are seen on a deep level. The process of creating is deeply healing too—for some people, it can heal trauma and depression, even if no one else ever sees it.[1] If we do share art with other people, it connects us with a community of other artists, which helps us feel like we're part of the world. When art is a hobby, it can be so fun to play as we create and get in touch with our younger selves, which are often freer. Creativity is considered a vital part of a healthy lifestyle, especially because it relieves stress and anxiety. And if you create for your work or a business, it can allow you to do the work you love the most.

Another reason why you should consider becoming an artist is because it changes you, just like being a magickal practitioner does. Whether it's on a small scale or a grand one, the very act of creating makes you stronger in ways you never knew were possible. Creativity is a higher-level energy experience. Being in the flow feels transcendent, almost like an otherworldly state. Art is one of the best ways to facilitate self-actualization, in my opinion. Creative life just feels more empowered compared to ordinary living. The highs of creativity simply don't compare to not creating.

Whether you have a specific idea in mind or you're starting from scratch, this book can help you engage in the magickal act of creation. It has the system that I developed over a few decades, which works for me in all my creative endeavors. Every chapter has both mundane and magickal information that will help you deepen your creative process and find the creative spirit. The magickal practices are simple, and rapid results are preferred so the focus can remain on your creative project.

Part 1 of this book reveals the beginning of the creative process to potential artists and encourages them to get into the

---

1. Cathy A. Malchiodi, *Art Therapy Sourcebook* (Los Angeles: Lowell House, 1998), xiii–xv.

mindset and habit of creating. The first chapter uncovers the spirits who inspire creation as well as the relationship that artists have with them. Next, the elements encourage you to act. Air inspires you to explore ideas and create an artistic vision. Fire sparks your passions and burns away any extraneous thoughts. Water washes away your fears of creating and promotes balance and the flow state. Earth encourages you to ground your idea into a physical form. The last chapter of part 1 uses the concept of a magickal circle to motivate you to complete a rough draft of your project. This could be a big endeavor, like your first try at writing a book, recording a demo of an album, ideas for a series of mixed-media paintings, the head-to-toe sketches of your fashion line, and so forth. Your project could also be smaller in scope, such as a performance of a three-minute song or making a few pieces of pottery with a specific theme or color.

Each of the chapters in part 1 has a simple ritual aspect that builds upon the ones that came before. This process is known as "habit stacking," and it's a highly effective way to accomplish goals and inspire good artistic habits.[2] I call these steps *the creative ritual*, and they cue the creative process to begin unfolding. This process works much of the time because it makes a pathway in the brain, which you can follow to get into your artistry. Science backs this up too. People who have rituals for their creative work are generally more successful than those who don't.[3] Using the creative ritual decreases the amount of willpower it takes to begin making art. Over time, it can lead us into the creative flow

---

2. James Clear, *Atomic Habits: An Easy and Proven Way to Build Good Habits & Break Bad Ones* (New York: Avery, 2018), 74–78.

3. Cal Newport, *Deep Work: Rules for Focused Success in a Distracted World* (New York: Grand Central Publishing, 2016), 100–58.

much faster than without it. It's especially helpful for beginner artists and people trying their hand at arts they're not familiar with.

In part 2, you'll refine the rough draft of your project by using some of the principles of alchemy. You'll also learn about the guiding spirit of the art, which is known as the *egregore*. The other chapters in part 2 delve into performance, releasing your art into the world in the most magickal ways possible, and creative renewal.

I wrote this book to help all kinds of artists with their creative processes. The information is presented in a chronological manner, which works well for the creation process. The best way to use this book is to read it in its entirety before creating and reread it as you go. This will let you see the entire creative process with objectivity. It's like going on a road trip with a detailed map about what you'll see and experience along the way. Reading it before you create lets you anticipate your next steps, and it gives you solutions to many common problems before they arise. It could save you countless hours and the terrible feeling of being lost despite knowing where you want to go. When you've read the whole book and you're ready to create, reread the important parts of the books for helpful reminders, especially when you feel stuck. It can also help you feel a sense of accomplishment to graduate to the next chapter.

There are a few terms used in this book that are shorthand for broader subjects. The words *art* and *creation* are synonyms for all kinds of art. Likewise, the word *artist* is used for all kinds of creators. The term *creative spirit* is used for any spirit that assists with the creative process. By using this generic word, I hope to capture the essence of creative spirits that are outside the known realms, such as those in cultures without much or any recorded history. Some historical names are used in the context they were given from the source. If any of the specific creative spirits appeal to you, I suggest that you research them to find more information. The books in the bibliography may have more insights.

You may wonder what my magickal qualifications are for writing a book like this. I'm happy to have a few decades of experience with magickal awareness and spirit work. I was raised in a home filled with folk magic and superstition, and my mother worked a sly bit of magick, sometimes with the fae. Like many children, I was aware of energy and spirits, and I had several unexplainable experiences that can only be described as magickal. Astral projections in my early years made me aware of the hidden energetic nature of the world and the spirits that live among us. I saw all kinds of spirits—guardian spirits, mischievous goblins, laughing faeries in the woods, full apparitions of ghosts, and the Wild Hunt, running in the wind. When I was in my early twenties, I learned the structure of magickal workings from attending rituals led by Selena Fox, a Wiccan high priestess with Circle Sanctuary, at a festival called the Pagan Spirit Gathering. A busy load of college courses kept me from doing too much, but seeing the structure of a ritual allowed me to develop my own intuitive practice. Now, over two decades later, I'm an eclectic pagan witch and the author of *Intuitive Witchcraft, Air Magic*, and *Modern Witchcraft with the Greek Gods* (which I coauthored with Jason Mankey).

As far as artistic disciplines go, I've worked in nearly all of them. I was a professional fire dancer for over a decade. I put myself through graduate school by dancing with fire. For two years, I sang in a traveling variety show. Upon first moving to Seattle, I sold my zine of pagan poetry by the Pike Place Market to make rent money. Since those early days, I've also published two fiction books, a few short stories, and poems. My other creative interests include photography, graphic design, collage, acting, modeling, dance, knitting, pottery, and painting.

I've had a wide variety of experiences with showcasing my art too. One of the highlights of my fire dancing career was performing at a club owned by Prince on New Year's Eve. My other performance venues include a pep rally at a packed high school auditorium, elite country clubs, a sex club, several glamorous gala events, wedding receptions, music festivals, a library, several backyards, and more city streets than I can count. My art has been displayed in high-production events and juried shows as well as gritty underground venues and snowy sidewalks. There were times when I had a director or a teacher to guide me, and many times, it worked well. Other times, they had their own ideas, which differed greatly from mine. Many of my artistic endeavors came about by training myself. I read books, watched videos of people doing the craft, and researched everything I could so I could bring my vision to life.

Throughout all these artistic experiences, I incorporated magick into my art. For me, creating is a deeply magickal act, and the more I treated it as such, the more magickal it became. I feel it's easy to incorporate more energy into creative endeavors—it's as simple as knitting protective intentions into a scarf, writing poetry for your magickal invocations and rituals, and painting with an emotion brought to the fore of your heart while you hold the paintbrush.

I felt inspired to write this book because I've had so many magickal experiences with the creation process that changed my life for the better. From my experience, I know that magick is the perfect medium to explore creative energy. Every act of creation changes the world. Artists are magicians, and I feel that artists use magick every time they change the materials that exist in their raw state into a finished work of art that people can understand and feel. They use magick every time they reveal unseen aspects of the energetic world in their art. Another thing I know for certain is that the creative process is utterly magickal. It's more than just creating and producing external works. Making art transforms artists into more magickal people.

As your creative process unfolds, I invite you to enjoy it. It takes courage to enter the strange worlds of your imagination, to climb metaphorical mountains of work, and to battle your critics, both inner and outer. However, with the right knowledge, the application of skills, and the creative ritual, you'll eventually come through the creative journey with your very own magickal art, which is more valuable than gold.

PART ONE

The Creative Spirit and the Creative Ritual

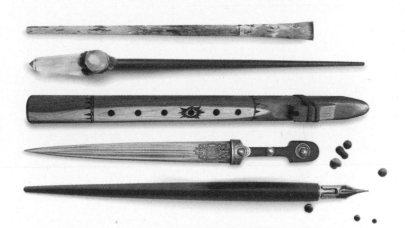

CRAFTING YOUR ROUGH DRAFT

CHAPTER 1

Creative Spirits: Inspiring Art

Creative spirits of all kinds have inspired artists to create brilliant pieces of art since the dawn of humanity. With their influence, countless works of art have been created, some of which are so perfect that they seem more like magickal conjurings than something made by human hands. It's fitting to have the creative spirits open this book, in all their forms and names, because creative spirits are with us before we even begin to create. It's also appropriate because some cultures believe it's important to acknowledge them and give thanks before creating, especially before starting a new project.

This chapter has information about the different kinds of creative spirits that can assist you with your creative endeavors, how they can inspire you, and how you can interact with them. Much of what we know about them comes from writers simply because they generally record their thoughts more often compared to artists such as dancers or sculptors. However, the information in this chapter is relatable for all kinds of creators.

The Many Spirits of Creativity

The spirits associated with creativity are well-known throughout Western history. Their primary role is to inspire artists by facilitating the flow of creative energy into them. Although there are many different names for them and the cultures they came from viewed them in unique ways, their similarities outnumber their differences. You'll probably recognize many of the spirits in this section because they've survived into the modern era, often with their fascinating lore intact.

THE MUSES

The Muses are probably the most popular creative spirits for artists in the modern era. Their first known reference came from about 2,800 years ago in ancient Greek poems written by Homer and Hesiod. The Muses are a collective of nine goddesses who govern different arts and sciences. Some people believe they represent the keys or channels through which the energy of the gods flows into artists, which is called inspiration. The word *muse* comes from the Greek word *mousa*, which means "song." This musical reference is reinforced by Hesiod, who said they gave him the gift of song and a mission to record Greek history in poetic hymns. The ancient Greeks believed that poets received transmissions from the Muses as they composed the poetry and as they performed it.[4]

The Muses' parents are Zeus, who is the most powerful patriarch of the Greek pantheon and is associated with divine thought, and Mnemosyne, the Titan goddess of memory. Considering that Mnemosyne came from an older generation of deities, it's possible that the Muses were known by people long before ancient Greek times. This kind of divine parentage fits that of colonial Greek expansion, when Zeus took the place

4. Gregory Nagy, "Hesiod and the Ancient Biographical Traditions," Harvard Center for Hellenic Studies, November 2, 2020, https://chs.harvard.edu /curated-article/gregory-nagy-hesiod-and-the-ancient-biographical -traditions/.

of a conquered god. The conquered goddess was allowed to remain, usually with her children, except their myths changed so that they were fathered by Zeus. The Muses were considered extremely important to ancient Greek society. The arts they inspired reiterated the Greek gods' relevance as well as the hierarchy. These aspects were clear in all parts of ancient Greek life—in day-to-day life, religious ceremonies, and the entertainment they inspired. The Muses include the following:

Calliope: The muse of epic poetry, whose name means "beautiful voice." She is chief of all the Muses and the mother of Orpheus, the greatest musician in Greece. She also governs creative writing.

Cleo: The muse of proclamations, history, and fame. She takes pleasure in recording the deeds of great people.

Erato: The passionate muse of song lyrics and love poetry. Her name is related to Eros, the god of love, as well as eroticism.

Euterpe: The muse of joyful works like music, singing, and poetry.

Melpominae: The chanting muse. She is associated with tragic plays, the Greek chorus, and religious celebrations involving dance and song.

Polyhymnia: The singer of many praises. She is the muse of sacred music, religious lyrics, dance, poetry, agriculture, math, and reflection. She is sometimes called the muse of mindfulness due to many depictions of her thinking pensively.

Terpsychorae: The muse of dance and rhythm.

Thalia: The muse of comedy. She is one of the most well-loved muses, and her name means "to flourish." Thalia presided over comic plays and idyllic poetry, including the *Odyssey* and the *Iliad*.

Urania: The celestial muse of astronomy, the earth, the stars, and unconditional love.

Over time, with shifting power dynamics and mixing cultures and beliefs, the concept of the Muses changed. The Romans acknowledged only three muses (Melete, which means "practice"; Mneme, "memory"; and Aoide, "song"). Belief in the Muses may have ceased altogether until the Renaissance Era. Around this time, the definition of a muse evolved to include actual people who inspired art. William Shakespeare, the playwright and poet, wrote about his muses, many of which are almost certainly people and not goddesses.

Sadly, the term *muse* has been used as a diminutive title, usually for women artists, as far back as the ancient Greek poet Sappho. The use implies that women are not real artists, but instead, they should play a supportive role to male artists by giving them inspiration and encouragement. Due to the complicated nature of this type of relationship, the human meaning for muse is not intended in this book, and no other references to the muse or the creative spirit carry that meaning.

Centuries later, several poets of the Romantic era in the nineteenth century penned poems to muses as creative spirits, including Emily Dickinson, Lord Byron, Percy Bysshe Shelley, and John Keats. In more modern times, many people cite the Muses as the source of their inspiration and success. For example, the horror writer Steven King called his writing companion his muse, and Tori Amos, musician and writer, said that conversing with them is part of her creative process.[5]

ANGELS AND DEMONS

The word *demon* has a long and varied history. It has been used as a catchall for a wide range of spirits—for everything from angelic guardian spirits to chaotic, mischievous spirits who cause ruin. The English word *demon* originated from the Greek *daimon*, which is generally defined as a powerful occult spirit that acts as an intermediary between humans and gods. Hesiod saw daimons as helpful ancestral spirits. For him, they were guardians and bringers of wealth.[6] Centuries later, Plato wrote his beliefs that at birth, each child received an *agathos daimon,* a benevolent guardian spirit who accompanied them. He saw the daimon as a piece of the divine mind that guided a human throughout their life and enacted their fate, in a way.[7] He also believed the daimon's nature was formed by the astrology at the time of birth, and that upon death, daimons accompanied souls to the underworld.[8] Daimons are mentioned frequently in the ancient Greek grimoire known as the *Papyri Graecae Magicae.* In it, there are rituals and spells to make them perform tasks for the magician

5. Stephen King, "The Writing Life," *Washington Post*, October 1, 2006, https://www.washingtonpost.com/wp-dyn/content/article/2006/09/28/AR2006092801398_pf.html; Pam Shaffer, interview with Tori Amos, *Why Not Both*, podcast audio, October 27, 2021, https://anchor.fm/why-not-both/episodes/Ep-95-Tori-Amos-e198uoj.

6. Walter Burkert, *Greek Religion*, trans. John Raffan (Cambridge: Harvard University Press, 1985), 180–81.

7. Burkert, *Greek Religion*, 328.

8. Plato, *Essential Dialogues of Plato*, trans. Benjamin Jowett (New York: Barnes & Noble Classics, 2005), 365.

who commanded them, and some of the work charged to them was nefarious. There don't appear to be any creative spells in that grimoire—the reason behind that may be due to the low literacy rate among artists and artisans at the time.

The Greek word *daimon* evolved to become the Roman word *daemon*, which was used as a helpful guardian spirit, like an angel. In Medieval times, the English term *demon* arose, and all the helpful connotations were removed. Instead, demons were synonymous with the devil, witches, oracles, magick, and the witch's familiar.

George Orwell, the writer of books such as *1984* and *Animal Farm*, called his creative spirit a demon. He said, "One would never [write a book] if one were not driven by some demon whom one can neither resist nor understand."[9] This indicates that demons assist with creativity in one way or another, perhaps as the creative spirit for some people. Angels are also cited by many modern artists as helpers along the creative journey.

THE GENUIS AND THE JUNO

The *genius* is another commonly known creative spirit. Much of the meaning of the genius seems to have come from the agathos daimon. The Romans believed each boy had a genius and each girl a *juno*, which arrived in the world with them at the moment of their birth. On birthdays, the person and their genius were both celebrated. The Roman concept of the genius eventually influenced the concept of guardian angels in Christianity.[10]

---

9. George Orwell, *Why I Write* (New York: Penguin Group, 2005), 10.

10. Gordon Jenning Laing, *Survivals of Roman Religion* (New York: Cooper Square Publishers, 1963), 23–24.

The word *genius* survived into the Enlightenment era, but at that time, its meaning changed to signify a person who was brilliant, artful, clever, or talented. Recently, the bestselling writer Elizabeth Gilbert, author of *Eat, Pray, Love,* repopularized the concept of the genius as a creative spirit in her 2009 TED talk and her book *Big Magic.*[11]

THE DUENDE

The *duende* is a creative spirit originally from Spanish and Portuguese cultures that gives artists the ability to express their deepest emotions through passionate performances. It's said to rise into performers through the soles of their feet. The poet Federico García Lorca viewed the duende as a daemon-like spirit of the earth that could be called forth from the deepest parts of an artist. He said that anyone who witnesses a performance with duende is struck by an overwhelming sense of power and mystery.[12]

The word *duende* translates to "ghost or goblin" in Spanish. It's related to the phrase *dueño de la casa,* which means "owner of the house."[13] This spirit-house relationship may be a metaphor for the duende spirit that exists within the artist. The writer Clarissa Pinkola Estés says the duende is the ability to use another spirit along with one's own, a "wind that blows soul into the

---

11. Elizabeth Gilbert, "Your Elusive Creative Genius," filmed February 2009 at TED2009, TED video, 19:15, https://www.ted.com/talks/elizabeth _gilbert_your_elusive_creative_genius/transcript.

12. Federico García Lorca, *In Search of Duende* (New York: New Directions Books, 1998), 49.

13. *Merriam-Webster,* s.v. "duende (*n.*)," accessed October 11, 2022, https:// www.merriam-webster.com/dictionary/duende.

faces of listeners," and a goblin wind.[14] The word *goblin* appears to describe the spirit-like energy of the duende, and in this case it probably doesn't relate to mischievous goblins popular in faery lore.

THE FAMILIAR

Many modern witches and magickal practitioners work with familiar spirits, which are sometimes thought of as guardian animal spirits, the fae, or forces of nature. These invisible beings help people with all kinds of magick, including divination, manifestation, and protection. Sometimes they even accompany their people into the otherworlds. The word *familiar* is derived from the Latin words *famulus* and *familiaris*, which mean household servant, though it appears this meaning came from the Church.[15] The term was popularized in the witch hunts and disparaged as satanic. Since the witchcraft revival in the 1960s, the familiar has been reclaimed as a helper spirit. Among modern practitioners, it's sometimes used synonymously with a witch's spirit guide or ally.[16] This helpful spirit can extend into our creativity, and some modern art witches use familiars in their creative process.

THE DEVIL AND DIVINITY

There's a lot of creative lore associated with the devil. Many of the stories include a person trading their soul for creative brilliance or worldly success. The oldest version of this story might have come from the story behind the *Codex Gigas*, or Devil's Bible,

14. Clarissa Pinkola Estés, *Women Who Run With the Wolves* (New York: Ballantine Books, 1995), 18, 480.

15. Raven Grimassi, *The Witch's Familiar: Spiritual Partnership for Successful Magic* (St. Paul, MN: Llewellyn Publications, 2003), 2–8.

16. Devin Hunter, *The Witch's Book of Spirits* (Woodbury, MN: Llewellyn Publications, 2017), 61.

the largest medieval book ever created. Legend has it that in the early 1200s, someone tried to create the entire book in a single night. When they realized they couldn't do it before dawn, they enlisted the help of the devil.[17] It may have inspired the story of Doctor Faustus, a man who traded his soul to the devil for his desires. This story originated in various forms in the late 1500s, and it was retold many times in the centuries afterward. The link to creative mastery came later in the Romantic era, when poets such as John Milton, William Blake, and Lord Byron were thought to be either sponsored by the devil or inspired by him as a muse.[18] Later, in the early 1800s, the composer and violin virtuoso Niccolò Paganini was said to have made a deal with the devil for his immense talent, which was said to be unnaturally beautiful. Nearly a century and a half later, in 1947, art imitated life when the relationship between the devil and the artist was retold in yet another Doctor Faustus rewrite by Thomas Mann, which featured a musical composer who traded his soul for true creative brilliance.

Another story with the same trope is the legend behind the blues musician Robert Johnson (1911–1938). He was a novice guitar player who disappeared for several months. When he reemerged, his contemporaries proclaimed him to be one of the greatest musicians of his time. Rumor had it that he got his talent by practicing in graveyards and by going to the crossroads, kneeling on the ground, and giving his guitar to the devil in exchange for his soul. His lyrics seem to contradict the devil aspect

17. "The Codex Gigas," Kungl Biblioteket, accessed June 18, 2022, https://www.kb.se/in-english/the-codex-gigas.html; "History of the Codex Gigas," Kungl Biblioteket, accessed June 18, 2022, https://www.kb.se/in-english/the-codex-gigas/history-of-the-codex-gigas.html.

18. Fred Parker, *The Devil as Muse* (Waco, TX: Baylor University Press, 2011), 2.

and instead attribute his talent to a deity. The lyrics of his song "Cross Road Blues," describe him kneeling at the crossroads and praying—not to the devil, but to "the Lord above."[19] Both forces are attributed as the source of his talent.

The core theme of these tales is trading a soul to the devil for artistic brilliance. This is notably different from the other lore surrounding the creative spirit. However, when the devil is put into the context of the Church's viewpoint, it starts to look more similar. For the Church, interaction with any spirits other than angels will make a person's soul corrupted. Of course, there's substantial evidence that suggests the Church combined a variety of pagan gods to create many facets of the devil.[20] In this light, the trade with the devil is less about the devil owning an artist's soul and more about the Church parting ways with artists who interacted with spirits or pagan gods. It becomes even clearer when you consider that the spirit offers the artist values the Church didn't approve of, including the realization of earthly desires, occult knowledge, success, wealth, and fame.

The devil in these tales begins to look identical to the creative spirit, especially because the Muses were associated with greatness and creative success. Homer, Hesiod, and Plato all believed this, and it was reiterated by countless artists over the next couple of millennia. Plato and Socrates believed the muse acted as an intermediary between us and a divinity who provided

19. Brian Oakes, dir., *ReMastered: The Robert Johnson Story* (Scotts Valley, CA: Netflix Originals, 2019).

20. Jason Mankey, *The Horned God of the Witches* (Woodbury, MN: Llewellyn Publications, 2021), 20.

inspiration.[21] This kind of activity describes the roles played by the Church's definition of spirits known as angels and demons.

Circling back to the concept of the deal made at the crossroads, several deities are associated with crossroads. Hermes and Mercury, the Greek and Roman messengers of the gods, were associated with writing and language. To this day, you can find relics and shrines made to them at ancient crossroads. Another crossroad deity is Hekate, the Greek goddess of magick, who was credited with the magickal transformations that happened there in exchange for an offering or a sacrifice. For a list of deities from various pagan pantheons and the arts they inspired, see the appendix.

Roman spirits who presided over the crossroads were known as the *lares compitales*. Since Roman times, people made countless shrines to them with offerings and candles that were left to burn through the night. This practice lasted into the late 1800s in many parts of Italy, if not longer, despite the Church's insistence on using saints there instead.[22]

In a similar vein to trading one's soul with the devil for creative success, some artists recommend making a deal with divinity. The authors of *The Artist's Way* encourage artists to make a powerful deal with the "creative force," whom they believe is a gender-neutral god or entity who is also known as "The Great Creator," the energy of flow, and one's "higher power."[23] Other people attribute deities to be a compelling source of inspiration. Jason Mankey, a pagan and witchcraft author, said, "The gods

---

21. Plato, *Essential Dialogues of Plato*, 11.

22. Laing, *Survivals of Roman Religion*, 21–23.

23. Julia Cameron and Mark Bryan, *The Artist's Way: A Spiritual Path to Higher Creativity* (New York: Putnam, 1992), xi–xii, 160.

push the pen.…There's a force that propels [writers] forward."[24] Considering all the blurred lines between these spirits, the devil, and deities, it's entirely probable that some people can interpret the creative spirit as the devil or a divinity.

ANCESTORS AND THE BELOVED DEAD

The ancient Greeks believed ancestral spirits and deceased heroes helped people with their problems. This belief has trickled down through the ages, sometimes with these spirits inspiring people with their creative endeavors. The group of artists known as the Shaker painters of the early 1800s believed that their powerful ancestors, saints, and leaders directly inspired them to create. Later, some artists of the Spiritualism movement, which began in the 1840s, also communicated with the dead to make art. The artist Augustin Lesage first began his artistic explorations during a séance, after which he was guided by the voices of the dead to create.[25] Not only can the spirits of the dead inspire the creation of art—they can also share revelatory knowledge about the mysteries of death and the underworld.

THE FAE

The fae or faery spirits are highly associated with the arts. It's rumored that all the great Celtic musicians learned how to play so well by going to the realm of the fae and learning from

---

24. Devin Hunter, "S9E19: Casting Spells with Jason Mankey," *Modern Witch*, March 25, 2022, MP3 audio, 10:32–10:44, https://podcasts.apple.com /us/podcast/s9e19-casting-spells-with-jason-mankey/id365213280?i =1000555262769.

25. S. Elizabeth, *The Art of the Occult: A Visual Sourcebook for the Modern Mystic* (London: White Lion Publishing, 2020), 195.

them.[26] The fae inspire poets too. The Irish spirits known as the *leanhaun sidhe* are thought of as muses, and they inspire poets to write. However, their relationships with the artists they inspire are so intensely amorous that the poets feel hunted by them, and they die at young ages. Faeries have also been known to inspire dancing.

The French painter Albert Maignan associated muses with the fae. His art nouveau painting *La Muse Verte* translates to "The Green Muse." It depicts a creative spirit inspiring a poet. The spirit has a double meaning. The liquor known as absinthe was called the "green fairy," and it inspired several well-known artists, including Picasso, van Gogh, Degas, Manet, and Toulouse-Lautrec.[27]

The fae have been associated with benevolent gifts, mischief, and malicious acts against humankind. It's generally agreed upon by most people that the fae don't observe the same social rules as humans. Some people have bad luck with them, but other people, like me, have a great relationship with them. If you're interested in them, use caution and do additional research to be sure they're a good fit.

AWEN

The Welsh word *awen* means "flowing spirit," and it's the personification of inspiration. It literally is thought of as perpetual energy, which humans experience inconstantly. Awen is associated with visions, a creative frenzy, and devotion, and it's felt most strongly by bards and poets.

---

26. Tom Cowan, *Fire in the Head* (New York: HarperCollins, 1993), 76–79.
27. "The Many Famous Artists Inspired by Absinthe," Absinthia, May 11, 2022, https://absinthia.com/blogs/absinthias-blog/the-many-famous -artists-who-have-been-inspired-by-absinthe.

CHANNELED SPIRITS

During the Spiritualism movement, many artists were inspired to channel spirits, to one degree or another, as they created. The artist Georgiana Houghton said she channeled her art with several spirit guides, whom she called her invisible friends.[28] Likewise, the artist Madge Gill entered a trance and became possessed by a spirit whose energy she drew from before she created. Some people in this movement allowed the spirit to have total control, and others cocreated with it. A few of these artists were considered spirit artists or artist mediums, including the painter Hilma af Klint.

THE SUBCONSCIOUS

Some artists from the Spiritualism and surrealism movements practiced automatism or automatic art by loosening their conscious minds and allowing their subconscious selves to create. Artists such as Salvador Dalí and Joan Miró tapped into a stream of inspiration that existed within them to make their fantastical art. While it's possible that your subconscious spirit can be your creative spirit, consider the possibility that the subconscious can communicate with the creative spirit better than the waking mind. Either one of these explanations is acceptable if it works for you. I believe it's up to personal interpretation of the phenomena. In any case, it explains why artists receive so many messages in the liminal moments between sleep and waking— these are the times when the subconscious is more active.

---

28. Pam Grossman, *Waking the Witch* (New York: Simon and Schuster, 2019), 161–63.

How Creative Spirits Help Artists

There are several theories about exactly how creative spirits help artists. Generally, the creative spirits are thought to conduct creative energy into artists. With their influence, artists can break through the limitations of their minds to create something amazing.

One of the most common concepts about creative spirits is that they inspire us to make art by breathing ideas into us. This process is clear when you look at the meaning of the word *inspire*, which means to breathe upon or to blow into.[29] Artists often feel inspired by the creative spirit. The people who enjoy art are inspired as well, especially when they encounter something beyond what they could have imagined on their own.

The roots of this word are present in Greek myth—Hesiod believed the Greek muses breathed their divine song into him.[30] This process suggests a flow of energy in both the form of a song and a cocreation process of the artist and the creative spirit.

Several other artists echo this kind of embodiment of the spirit and cocreation. They say their sense of self dissolves to some degree, and the creative spirit and the artist act together. This could be described as possession or channeling. For artists, these words usually indicate the process of allowing a spirit to use their bodies, to some degree. Tori Amos reiterates this concept: "When we're channeling our muses, then we realize we're

29. Online Etymology Dictionary, s.v. "inspire (*v.*)," accessed October 11, 2022, https://www.etymonline.com/word/inspire.

30. Apostolos N. Athanassakis, trans., *Theogony, in Hesiod: Theogony, Works and Days, Shield*, 2nd ed. (Baltimore, MA: Johns Hopkins University Press, 2004), lines 30–34.

in collaboration with them, and we're really like a vessel."[31] Like-wise, the poet Alisha Ostraker wrote about cocreating with the creative spirit: "The voice...entered me...and somehow or other, we produced the words."[32] In these cases, the artist and creative spirit are both present and creating simultaneously.

There are many examples of this kind of artistic possession. The Shaker painters thought of themselves as instruments through which spirits could take control of their bodies and paint. Plato believed that all good poets experienced divine possession by the Muses: "[Good poets] are inspired and possessed....There is no invention in him until he has been inspired and is out of his senses, and the mind is no longer in him."[33] Plato went on to say that even if an artist knows all the artistic techniques and has a high degree of rationality, they will always be eclipsed by the mad, muse-possessed artist. He considered the ecstasy of inspiration to be a divine gift that was like the feeling of falling in love. Anyone who has drawn a spirit or a deity into their body may be familiar with this sensation.

Some artists hear their creative spirit. Ray Bradbury, the writer of *Fahrenheit 451* and many other books, credited every-thing he wrote to a demon muse who whispered in his ear and

31. Pam Shaffer, "Ep 95: Tori Amos," October 27, 2021, in *Why Not Both*, pro-duced by Laura Studarus and Under the Radar magazine, podcast, MP3 audio, 19:47, https://anchor.fm/why-not-both/episodes/Ep-95-Tori -Amos-e198uoj.

32. "An Interview with Alicia Ostriker," *Nashville Review*, August 1, 2012, https://as.vanderbilt.edu/nashvillereview/archives/5452.

33. Plato, *Essential Dialogues of Plato*, 11.

told him what to write.[34] Likewise, the authors of *The Artist's Way*, Julia Cameron and Mark Bryan, wrote, "There is a second voice, a higher harmonic, adding to and augmenting your inner creative voice.…We can learn not only to listen but also to hear with increasing accuracy that inspired, intuitive voice that says, 'do this, try this, say this.'"[35] The voice often knows more than we do. Listening to it gives us insights we may never have gleaned on our own.

A few visual artists showed how they perceive the creative spirit's influence. Many depict it as an amicable but wholly occult touch from a spirit. In the painting *The Muse Inspiring the Poet*, Henri Rousseau depicts a friendly, womanly figure with her arm around another figure, the poet. The placement of the muse's left hand is not shown. It's somewhere behind the poet, which suggests a kind of puppetry happening around the poet's heart. Likewise, in the painting *Kiss of the Muse*, Paul Cézanne painted a winged, womanly muse kissing the forehead of a poet. This appears to show the transmission of the muse's inspiration into the mind of the poet. Furthermore, the location of the kiss is at the place commonly called the third eye or the witch's eye, a place of insight and timeless knowledge. In yet another variation of the creative spirit and the artist, the painting *The Green Muse* depicts a woman muse floating behind a man. She grasps his forehead commandingly, and her face has a mischievous look, as if she's taking pleasure in relating a story from another world to him.

---

34. Catherine Donaldson-Evans. "An Interview with Sci-Fi Legend Ray Bradbury," Fox News, last modified May 20, 2015, https://www.foxnews.com/story/an-interview-with-sci-fi-legend-ray-bradbury.

35. Cameron and Bryan, *The Artist's Way*, 118–119.

Some artists say their creative process is like traveling into another world. It seems that when you're creative, you're more open to the otherworld and you can interact with spirits more easily. Jonathan Zap, a science fiction writer, wrote that his muse drew back a curtain and revealed a portal to him. He entered that other world for inspiration and cocreation with his muse.[36] His experiences are written as if they actually happened, but that's not the case for everyone. For centuries, many people believed that the most brilliant Celtic musicians studied music in the faery realm, where they learned how to play and compose songs. In at least some of these instances, the realm of faery was not a physical location, but a mental or spiritual one. This inner kind of journey was not thought of as any greater or less than an actual physical journey. When Steven King said that his writing happened on two different levels simultaneously, he may have been alluding to operating in the physical realm as well as a spiritual/artistic one.

EXPERIMENTING WITH CHANNELING

Your relationship with the creative spirit will likely be influenced by your artistic medium and how comfortable you are with being open to it. You may want to channel the spirit and let it move through you, or you may want to retain some control. If you're interested in channeling, experiment with trance states and creating for long hours. Whenever you start to feel as if something is coming over you, lean into that feeling and allow your mind to continue along that path. Don't change too much about your cir-

---

36. Jonathon Zap, "The Path of the Numinous: Living and Working with the Creative Muse," Zap Oracle, March 19, 2014, https://zaporacle.com/the -path-of-the-numinous-living-and-working-with-the-creative-muse/.

cumstances—whatever brings the creative spirit to you is more important than how you may have envisioned it happening. When you feel a slight separation in your mind, body, or spirit, you'll know it's happening.

For each creative discipline, there's a different ideal combination of self to spirit. What works for making figurines, say 50 percent self and 50 percent creative spirit, may not work for dance, which may be closer to 20 percent self and 80 percent creative spirit. If you have multiple creative disciplines, you'll discover that the creative spirit feels a little different for each of the arts you do. It stimulates different areas of the body and mind with a wide range of sensations. When I was writing fiction, my mind felt as if it were buzzing with dozens of bees. Fire dancing is a whole other experience—the creative spirit moves around me like a partner, directing me and teasing out playful movements. Several levels of myself are present at this time, including my waking mind, subconscious, and higher self.

Try to find levels that are most conducive to your art and ones you're comfortable with. Ideally, you'll be able to experience the influence of the spirit and continue to create at the same time. You'll know when it's the right combination because it'll feel natural for the artistic medium. If possible, write down the ratio of self to spirit so you can make it happen again more easily. As you progress and gain more abilities, be open to changing the ratio. You may discover that you don't need to give as much control to the spirit or that you prefer to give them more.

Be sure to read the tips and best practices for working with spirits at the end of this chapter for information about how to proceed in a sustainable way. It also has instructions on how to protect yourself from malevolent spirits.

The Animalistic Creative Spirit

Many people believe the creative spirit looks human because that's how the Muses were depicted by Greek writers. This imagery lives on in modern art, especially in poetry and visual art. However, ancient writers also thought of the creative spirit as an animal. The Romans associated the genius with a snake, and the Greeks and the Romans both believed the agathos daimon took the form of a snake.[37] Canines were also popular forms for spirits to take. The Greek writer Pausanias wrote about a genius spirit who wore wolf skin, and the Roman writer Pierius compared genii to "sagacious dogs."[38] Even the Latin name of a domestic dog, *Canis familiaris*, seems to recall the familiar spirit.

The animalistic concept of the creative spirit appears to have survived from Roman times into the medieval era. *Muser*, the Medieval Latin word from which the English word *muse* is derived, means "mouth of an animal."[39] The animalistic concept of a helpful spirit may have influenced how people viewed the witch's familiar, which included several animals, but mostly snakes, dogs, cats, toads, rats, ferrets, rabbits, bats, and birds, especially ravens and owls.[40]

Steven King believed every artist had "one small animal" who helped them create. "There is indeed a half-wild beast that lives in the thickets of each writer's imagination," he wrote. "Scruffy

---

37. Laing, *Survivals of Roman Religion*, 26–27.

38. John Beaumont, *An Historical, Psychological, and Theological Treatise of Spirits, Apparitions, Witchcrafts, and other Magical Practices* (London: D. Browne, 1705), 17–19.

39. *Merriam-Webster*, s.v. "muse (*n.*)," accessed October 11, 2022, https://www.merriam-webster.com/dictionary/muse.

40. Grimassi, *The Witch's Familiar*, 1.

little mutt has been around for years, and I love her....She gives me the words."[41] Although dogs are popular choices for creative spirits, creative spirits take many other animalistic forms, like my gentleman crow spirit.

I believe an artist's pet can also assist them with their creative endeavors by contributing their energy to the creative process. My cat loves to be near me when I write. Sometimes, I wonder if he's supporting my writing by being so close to me. Our pets may play a part in attracting the creative spirit to us. Curiously, my creative spirit only appeared to me visually after I adopted my cat from a local shelter. Their animalistic, wild spirits might be sympathetic to one another, which works in our favor.

How You Might Experience the Creative Spirit

People describe their experiences with the creative spirit in a variety of ways. Your medium of art will likely inform how you'll experience the creative spirit. A musician's creative spirit is likely to be vocal and inspire them with sounds compared to a visual artist, whose creative spirit might never make a sound, but could show them intriguing visual concepts as well as thoughts about certain colors and shapes.

ECSTATIC ENERGY

For some artists, the presence feels ecstatic. There's a sense of joy, excitement, and sometimes even nervousness. Some artists say their presence feels like heat, and others say it feels cool. Many report the sensation of dissolving and an awareness of the otherworld. Elizabeth Gilbert said her experience with the creative

41. King, "The Writing Life."

process felt "downright paranormal."[42] For some artists, such as the poet and writer Opal Palmer Adisa, creativity and sensuality are combined to create an utterly inspirational frenzy. She calls her muse both "lover" and "Eros," and her writing has luscious accounts of her interactions with it.[43]

THE OCCULT HELPER

It seems that the creative spirit doesn't like to be looked at, at least not at first. My experience of seeing my creative spirit disappear mirrors that of many other artists across multiple disciplines. Even some of the most prolific artists have this experience. Steven King said his muse is "not used to being regarded so directly," and Federico García Lorca said he only saw his muse twice.[44] The elusive nature of the spirit makes sense if you consider that it could be part of the large collective of occult spirits. Of course, some of the definitions of the word *occult* include "hidden from view," "not easily understood," and "not revealed."[45] If this is the case, the creative spirit may not be shy as much as it's hidden by nature.

If you've ever seen any spirits before, you'll probably have a predisposition to see your creative spirit. When it first appears to you, remain focused on your art and observe it from the corner of your sight. Over time, they'll likely reveal more of themselves to you.

---

42. Gilbert, "Your Elusive Creative Genius."

43. Opal Palmer Adisa, *Eros Muse: Poems and Essays* (Trenton, NJ: Africa World Press, 2006), 143.

44. King, "The Writing Life"; Lorca, *In Search of Duende*, 50.

45. *Merriam-Webster*, s.v. "occult (*adj.*)," accessed June 1, 2022, https://www.merriam-webster.com/dictionary/occult.

THE EVOLVING CREATIVE SPIRIT

The creative spirit can change over time as you build trust with it. You may notice that they change their appearance, size, color, and other characteristics. My creative spirit became less of a lurker and more of an expressive friend after a few sessions. He started to cheer me on animatedly and hop around in excitement whenever we wrote something particularly good. With every session, he grew larger too. There were times when he towered behind me like a seven-foot shadow. However, I noticed that when I put my project down, he shrunk back to his cat-size self.

I believe that spending time with your creative spirit will reveal more about both of your personalities. It's also possible that this relationship strengthens the spirit, and because of that, they can change their form or appearance. Go with the flow as they reveal more of themselves to you through your creative journey. What they look like isn't as important as the relationship, the inspiration they give you, and the art you create together.

DREAM COMMUNICATIONS

Creative spirits often communicate with us in dreams. It's much easier for them to talk with us this way because when we're close to sleep, we're in a deeply liminal state. To make the most of this liminal magick, keep a blank book and a pencil by your bed, and write down your dreams as soon as you wake up. Even if you only have one memory upon waking, write it down. Sometimes, you may only wake with a feeling or a color from the dream, and that's enough to connect us with that realm. The most ephemeral detail can unlock more information, but you often have to write down the first part before more can come through. I believe that recording anything you remember about your dreams gives you stronger connections with those liminal states and the creative part of the brain. This practice also forms beneficial connections between our waking minds and the creative otherworlds that exist both within us and outside of us.

When you don't remember your dreams, don't worry. This is a normal part of life, and it may be a normal part of the creative process too. I believe the creative spirit helps us in our dreams even when we don't remember anything about them.

There are a few ways you can use your dream connection with your creative spirit to strengthen the bond between you. When you're ready to go to sleep, take a moment to invite them to meet you in your dreams. If it works, it's a fun activity that helps you familiarize yourselves with each other. You can also take a moment to ask them for help solving a problem in your dreams. When you're on good terms with your spirit, ask them to reveal their name in a dream. If you do learn their name, I recommend keeping it private. There's a lot of spirit lore that says that knowing a spirit's real name gives someone the power to command them. Whether this is true or not, you might as well be safe and keep it to yourself. If you decide to talk about them with other people, you can always use a dummy name to protect them.

VISIONS OF ART

One theory about creative spirits is that they want a specific kind of art in the world. They move through the world until they find an artist or multiple artists who can bring the vision to life, and they inspire them to accomplish it. This concept may have been at play in the sculpture works of the Renaissance artist Michelangelo, who said he saw the statues that were hidden within the blocks of stone, and his work merely liberated them. Likewise, the painter Jackson Pollock believed his paintings had lives of their own, and he merely let the art come through.

Elizabeth Gilbert experienced an astounding example of a creative spirit wanting a specific kind of art in the world. Much to her surprise, she discovered that she and a distant friend were both writing a story with strikingly similar details. There are many other stories about similar artistic duplications without communication with other artists. Inventors and engineers seem to have the problem a lot as well, and patents are sometimes denied due to remarkable similarities.

These stories suggest that the creative spirit may visit more than one artist at a time. It could also mean that a much larger spirit, such as a zeitgeist (a spirit of the times) or an egregore (a powerful psychic thought-form), can act as a driving force to help humanity create something they believe is necessary.

Your Creative Correspondences

We all have our own unique pathways and ritualistic items that help us find the creative spirit. I call these *creative correspondences*—they are all the things and situations that assist you in cultivating an artistic mindset and find your creative spirit. The word *correspondence* implies both magick and communication. When these meanings are applied to items, it means they'll help you find the right magickal energy for your art. Some examples of creative correspondences include songs, herbs, crystals, colors, times of day, seasons, and moods. I believe that these creative correspondences specifically allow us to communicate with the creative spirit so it can facilitate the flow of inspiration.

This belief is not only from personal gnosis—it also appears in ancient Greek literature. The first time that Hesiod found the

Muses, he had been herding his flock while walking through the mountainous ranges of Boeotia. He sought them again so he could accomplish what they charged him to do—to record the stories of the gods. Hidden within his offhand comment is a deeper narrative. The inspiration they gave him was so important that he became adept at finding them no matter where they appeared or where they fled. Some historians agree with his obsessive tendency, with one stating that Hesiod's "trysts with Mnemosyne and her nine daughters, the muses...were not chance encounters, but rather, complex arrangements that involved the mind."[46] Although Hesiod's exact steps to find the Muses again are unknown, he likely repeated the same things that worked the first time. He probably traveled along the same paths, made the same offerings, and arrived at the same place and the same time of day as before. He may have eaten the same food and wore the same clothing and jewelry. It's likely he spoke to the same gods, sang the same songs, and kept the same distance from his flock in the hopes of finding them again.

Creative correspondences are helpful, especially to newer artists, who often have difficulty finding the right mindset to sustain creation. Even accomplished artists need a bit of help now and then too. Creative correspondences are like catalysts—they provide a big boost of energy to help you get over the hump of potential energy and into an active creative process.

Other people advocate for creating a ritual in order to find the creative flow state. There are several scientific studies that back up the results of habit stacking, including in the creative arts. The pagan artist Mickie Mueller, author of *The Witch's Mirror* and *Llewellyn's Little Book of Halloween*, writes, "Adding the

46. Athanassakis, *Hesiod*, xiv.

element of ritual to the creation of my art has enabled me to connect on a spiritual level with the subject and channel that into the work."[47] Creative rituals give us a stepwise process for metaphorically walking down the path to find the creative spirit. They connect us with the spirit, give us successes, and keep us coming back so we can go even deeper into our art. In this light, it makes sense to ritualize your creative time, especially if you're a magickal practitioner of any kind.

You may already have items that help you create. If not, think about what helps you feel the mental spark of creativity. You'll get a chance to encounter creative correspondence items in the following elemental chapters, where you'll develop your own creative ritual. Each chapter will have several examples and the traditional meanings of objects you can try in your creative ritual. Feel free to use your own personal gnosis to determine what works best for you. This chapter has only one correspondence—spirit. With each elemental chapter afterward, you'll add nuance to your ritual to find the best energy for your creative process. Once you establish your set of creative correspondences, you'll forge a path in your mind so you can find the creative spirit again and again.

It is the Muses who have caused me to be honored: they taught me their craft.

—SAPPHO

As you grow with your talent and your art, be open to changing your creative correspondences and experimenting with different combinations. My creative correspondences came to me

---

47. Mickie Mueller, "The Magical Art of the Well Worn Path," Llewellyn, January 30, 2006, https://www.llewellyn.com/journal/article/1047.

after many years of trial and error with items and rituals. Whenever something worked, I used it again. If I felt it wasn't helping, I skipped it to see how well I did without it. Over time, I got better and better results, and that's when my creative spirit arrived. In hindsight, the connection was blatantly apparent once I found my path.

You may not need all the correspondences suggested in this book, but it doesn't hurt to try them out and drop the ones that don't work. Use whatever helps you communicate with the creative spirit, but keep in mind that these correspondences are for you, not them. Write down the creative correspondences that work for you so you can use them again and try to repeat the experience.

CREATIVE CORRESPONDENCES FOR SPIRIT: YOUR WORKPLACES

The correspondences for the creative spirit are your workplaces—both the physical area where you create *and* the mental/spiritual space within you. Think of these workplaces as ritual places that exist outside you and inside you. When both have been cleansed and prepared to encounter the creative spirit, you'll begin traversing the energetic path to find it. Clarissa Pinkola Estés writes, "If one prepares a special psychic place, then the being, the creative force, the soul force, will hear of it, sense its way to it, and inhabit that place."[48] This is the goal—to help the creative spirit come through more easily so the magick can begin. Please note that both of these workplaces are important. If you only have one of them ready for creative work, the spirit may not come, or it may only give you hints about what kind of art you could create.

---

48. Estés, *Women Who Run With the Wolves*, 298.

Think of your creative workplaces as the ritual spaces where the magick will happen. They're the sacred locations of your magickal art. You wouldn't stop a ritual to accept a phone call unless it was important, would you? Would you let a random visitor interrupt you? Mentally, you wouldn't allow yourself to dwell on something troubling in a ritual either—ideally, you'd be fully involved in the magickal process. That's the kind of thinking you'll need to cultivate. Your creative time is sacred, and it should be treated as such.

It's a good idea to minimize any distractions such as phone notifications so you can focus on your art without interruption. If that's not possible because you need to be reached in case of an emergency, change your phone settings to silence anyone outside of that list. Let your list know that during your creative time, they should only contact you if there's an emergency. You can reduce in-person interruptions by hanging a sign on your door. Use a simple phrase to dismiss visitors, like "Busy now. Come back later." If you'd like, you can leave a whiteboard and markers or some paper and pencils by the door so people can leave you a note.

When it's time to create, show up to your creative workspaces as you would with your magickal practices. Be alert, cleansed, and ready for magic. Plan to create after you've eaten a light meal. Don't do it when you're hungry or you've eaten so much that you feel lethargic. Be recently showered or bathed, and wear comfortable, clean clothes that inspire you to create. All these simple ritual preparations will help you cultivate the right mindset and attract the creative spirit. Your preparatory ritual doesn't have to be elaborate; otherwise, the immensity of it might intimidate you from showing up. Your daily shower, meals, and clothes will likely work out fine.

There are many nuances to every workplace, such as the time of day, the temperature of the room, the lighting (both the positioning and the color), your clothing, the furniture or decorations in your workplace, and even the weather. Experiment with your setup and see if different things give you more inspiration or focus. I found that an overhead lamp, a heater by my feet, and a cat curled up by my side during cool weather were among my creative correspondences associated with my workplace. When I had all of these in place, as well as my elemental creative correspondences, I could easily tune into my art. Although most people don't think of these things as stereotypical correspondences, they definitely helped me find the right energy because they created the right atmosphere, or container, for the magic.

• Ritual •
Cleansing a New Creative Workplace

Before you use your creative workplaces for the first time, cleanse them and dedicate them with an intention. Try out a couple of these options for cleansing your workplace before you use them for the first time with the creation proces. Use them again whenever the energy becomes stagnant or not helpful.

- Burn dried herbs such as rosemary, sage, bay leaves, or mugwort in a cauldron. Waft the smoke around the room and imagine all the stagnant energy dissipating.

- Light a few sticks of your favorite incense. Alternately, you can burn incense resin such as copal, myrrh, frankincense, dragon's blood, or pine on a charcoal disk set on sand in a cauldron.

- Make sigils for your workplace by combining a few pared-down images, letters, and symbols. I suggest creating one sigil that's protective and one that's supportive for you or your art.

- Make a jar of sunwater or moonwater by filling a glass jar and exposing it to the light of the sun or the moon. Sunwater supports daytime activities, direct energy, and personal power; and moonwater elevates night work, mysteries, depth, and feelings. Use this water to dust surfaces, anoint the door and windows with sigils, and mop the floor.

- Create a magickal and fragrant spray by adding several ounces of moonwater to a couple of drops of essential oils and vanilla extract in a spray bottle. Spray the air until the aroma fills the workplace. Please be aware that it's important to use caution when first using essential oils to determine whether an allergic reaction or irritation might occur. Use extra caution with oils of cinnamon, clove, oregano, thyme, and any citrus. Those are best used in minute doses, if at all, because they may be caustic or they may interfere with medicine. If you're pregnant, research all oils before using them to ensure safety.

- Make an oil blend by combining a couple of drops of essential oil in a couple of ounces of carrier oil, such as almond or jojoba. Use it to anoint yourself, your wooden furniture, and the door with sigils or other intentions.

- Cleanse your workplace during a special sun station, such as midsummer, or a moon phase, such as the new moon or the full moon. Ask for the energy of that celestial alignment to help you with your goals.

• If you work with a deity or a spirit, ask them for protection or a blessing upon your workplace.

After cleansing your space, cleanse yourself in a similar method, especially around your head, shoulders, and back. Think about the space that the creative spirit occupies within the mind and aura, and envision that place being cleared.

Next, cast a protective magickal circle in your preferred manner. Circles allow you to raise energy, retain energy, and protect against undesirable spirits. If you prefer a different method for protection, such as asking your spirit guide, using protective charms, or drawing sigils on the walls, use them. The more layers of protection, the better.

Take time to write an intention for the place. Include details that are relevant to you and leave it open-ended about the result so you have flexibility and the ability to change direction. Your intention may look something like this: "I dedicate these workplaces to the magickal art of making music. I invite the creative spirit to this circle. Spirit, I seek a beneficial relationship with you. Let's write beautiful songs together."

Spend a little time creating and getting a feel for the creative spirit. Afterward, give thanks and open the circle. You can cast a circle each time you create or not—it's up to you and how comfortable you feel in that space.

Continue to cleanse your creative workplaces regularly or whenever the energy is off. If you work in public areas such as coffeehouses or cafés, consider carrying protective items with you.

CREATIVE RITUAL: SPIRIT

Go to your art workplace. Minimize distractions. Organize your space—tidy up and do a light cleaning if it needs it. Get in your creating position, whether that's standing before an easel, sitting at a desk, or however you work. Take a few deep breaths and clear your mind. Feel the energy in the room. Welcome the creative mindset within you and be open to the presence of the creative spirit. If you wish, you can say hello.

• *Ritual* •
CALL UPON THE CREATIVE SPIRIT

Some artists call upon the creative spirit before they begin to create. Hesiod and Homer recited a few lines of poetry for the Muses at the beginning of their performances so the Muses would give them greater ability to deliver the stories. For some people, this ancient practice continues into modern days: writer Steven Pressfield recites Homer's *Invocation to the Muses* before he writes.[49] Many artists don't do this, and you don't need to call upon them for them to show up. However, it doesn't hurt to speak to them, especially if you're first getting to know them.

The best way to approach your relationship with the creative spirit is as a new friendship. Use caution at first and be friendly but not a pushover. Allow trust to be earned on both sides before opening your mind up to them completely. Speak to them aloud

---

49. Steven Pressfield, *The War of Art: Break Through the Blocks and Win Your Creative Battles* (New York: Black Irish Entertainment, 2012), 109–11.

and earnestly. I advise using respectful language and not using words like *summon* or *command*. Those words imply you have control over the spirit, and that may not actually be the case. It's far more polite to call upon the spirit or request its presence.

If you'd like something formal, you can either write an invocation to them or find one that someone else wrote. Try Homer's *Invocation* as a starting point. If you're interested in something more informal, you can simply call upon them and speak from the heart. Here's an example: "Creative spirit, hello. I invite you to join me. Today, I'm interested in creating (description of project)."

Start creating after you speak the invocation. Remember, the creative spirit likes focus, so give it something to be curious about so it'll stick around. When you're done, thank it by saying something like, "Thank you for all the inspiration you gave me today. I appreciate you, and I'll be back soon. Goodbye for now."

Best Practices with New Spirits

It's important to protect yourself against spirits who lie and mean harm to you. Whenever a spirit appears in your creative workplace, read its energy. If they seem malevolent, they don't seem interested in creativity, or they tell you flattering things you want to believe about yourself, they're probably not a creative spirit. The best course of action is to banish them from your workplace. To do so, first stand firm and feel your power deep in your bones, muscles, and blood. With a clear and strong voice, say something like, "I banish you from my creative workplace, spirit. Be gone from here!" In your mind's eye, imagine that you can see the spirit being whisked outside, somewhere away from you. Take a calming breath. Cleanse your space and return to your art.

If you believe you have attracted a creative spirit, make art with them over a few weeks to establish trust between you. Take it slow and don't expect too much from them when you're first starting. Be patient. Ideally, you will allow them to open up to you on their own time. They may want to evaluate how committed you are to your art, or they might want to see your artistic vision before they interact with you. Share your trust in your creative spirit, as long as it deserves it, and allow that bond to increase over time. Believe deep within yourself that you're worthy of interacting with them.

It's best to be mindful of the time when you're first interacting with them. Many hours can pass by quickly when you're under their spell. You can set an alarm for the time you'd like to stop working. Stick to that time and don't allow your art time to drain you completely. It's best to save some of your energy so you can get home, ground with food and water, and rest up.

Once you've experienced the creative spirit, decide how often this kind of interaction is healthy for you. The goal of working with them is not to become haunted by the desire to create, but rather, to be an artist who lives a balanced life with the added bonus of that special relationship. It's important to have a social life and to take care of yourself on every level—physically, emotionally, mentally, and spiritually. All these healthy everyday practices allow you to eventually create the right conditions to be open to their energy, and they help you sustain your sessions so you can build endurance.

If you get ideas for more than one project, you either have multiple creative spirits or your creative spirit is making everything attractive to you. During times like these, I've found it's best to go along with the loudest urge, which is usually the project you're the most passionate about or the one you keep getting ideas about. Regarding the other projects, simply take notes on them for possible later use. Keep in mind that you may also need to switch projects if another project seems to be more interesting to you or the creative spirit. It's easier to work with the flow of intrigue than against it.

Tips for Working with Creative Spirits

- Lose yourself in your art. Surrender to the creative trance whenever possible.

- Keep an open mind about what will happen. You may or may not see results right away. Allow it all to happen, and let the creative spirit inform the work rather than driving at your project with sheer mental or physical force. This means you may have to slow down to feel the energy move through you. When you do this, your art can take on a life of its own and inform you about your options.

- Sometimes, the creative spirit will call upon you in strange places. You may receive ideas when you're falling asleep, when you're in the shower, or when you've had a break from your art. Some of your ideas may not be relevant to the project at hand, and they won't leave your mind. These ideas have some of the juiciest insights. If you can switch projects to do the more exciting idea, do so. If you can't, take notes and circle back to them sometime soon.

- One way to attract the creative spirit is to purposefully do nothing and become bored. An empty mind with no preconceived notions might be one of the most useful ways to connect with the creative spirit.

- Hesiod found the Muses while walking in nature, and like him, we can get closer to them when we go outside. Take a walk to clear your mind and open yourself up to a trance state. Often, when we get into nature, we encounter the spirit of nature or the land, which can move through us much like the creative flow. To tune in, take in everything. Observe the sky and the landscape. Watch how the wind moves through the tree leaves and plants. Feel the heat of the sun or the coolness of the shadow. Lose yourself in something greater than yourself, even if it's just for a moment.

Spirited Away

An intimate connection with the creative spirit may seem far-fetched or impossible until you've actually experienced it. Your ability to show up and be open is vital, but these skills take time. Be patient with yourself and your creative spirit. If you've ever been deeply moved by art or any kind of performance, you can probably have this kind of relationship. Whenever you go to your creative workplace to create, you'll build the budding relationship between you and the creative spirit. As you read through the next few chapters in part 1, keep these concepts in mind so you can continue to enhance this inspirational connection.

CHAPTER 2

Air: Vision and Inspiration

Every creative project starts with the faintest whispers of inspiration. An idea enters the artist's mind and begins to develop and move them from within. Inspiration comes in so many forms—you could become quite taken by a certain shade of red on a fresh apple, a mysterious phrase that unlocks a strong feeling in your chest, or a song lyric that evokes an interesting character with a torrid backstory. Great artists focus on those glimmering micro-thoughts and the exciting feelings that come with them. They expand the ideas in their minds, and soon, connections begin to appear. Other bright thoughts come rushing in, filling in the blanks with sumptuous details. Just like magick, your art begins to take shape.

Air is often the first element called upon in ritual, and it's a good starting point for your creative projects too. It's associated with beginnings, mindset, focus, communication, and clarity. You'll use the active aspects of this element to set the stage for your ideas to come alive.

Cultivate the Mindset of an Artist

The best way to begin creating art is to attain an artist's mindset. I believe there are three tenets that create this supportive mentality.

With them, you can navigate the artist's journey with ease. Without them, you may never create anything.

The first tenet of the artist's mindset is to believe that you are an artist, even if you don't have any work to show for it. If you've only ever dreamed up art or thought, "This is how I would do it," you're an artist. Even if you've never finished anything, never went to art school, never had an art show, and never sold anything, you're still an artist.

If we go all the way back to the ancient world ... [people] are not thought to be authors so much as vessels through which other forces act and speak.

—Lewis Hyde

You don't have to make art to *be* an artist because artists aren't always creating. Sometimes, they're dreaming up new ideas. Other times, they're buying supplies or getting inspiration from visiting museums or recitals. Far more often, artists are doing things that aren't related to their creations whatsoever, such as dreaming, eating, grooming, talking with their loved ones, and doing some kind of work. My point is this: artists are still artists even when they're not creating because they're more than what they do. There's an inner artistic essence that exists within all of us. You just have to acknowledge the presence of it.

The second tenet to having an artist's mindset is to believe that you have the potential to create something, which is true. You have the ability to make something amazing! The fact that other people have created wonderful things means that you can do it too. It'll take work and dedication to learn about your craft, but if you're passionate enough, you'll make it happen. The next couple of chapters cover this in more detail, but for now, just believe that it's possible for you to create what you dream.

The third tenet for an artist's mindset is to daydream and not overthink the ideas that you get. Overthinking is the enemy of art and vision. Instead, put yourself into a resting state and let your ideas float into your mind. Many of these ideas come from the parts of our brains that take care of things automatically. This is called the default mode network of the brain, and it's associated with imagination, idle thought, daydreaming, and going on automatic pilot.[50] If you've ever driven from one place to another safely, and you forgot all the details about how you reached the place, you were operating under your default mode. You knew how to drive, and your mind knew how to guide you from one place to the other. The good news is that the default mode network does this with all kinds of ideas as well. This is why people get ideas in the shower.

Some people believe that the brain's default mode is similar to being in an animistic state, where you feel that everything has an energy and a spirit, and you go along with the flow of it all. This spirit-idea connection means that your default mind may make you more receptive to the creative spirit. To take advantage of this natural connection, allow your mind to rest and daydream on a daily basis. If you ever notice yourself spacing out, let your mind wander for a few minutes. It may come back with some interesting ideas.

The artistic mindset may take a while to sink in, but it's important to practice those tenets. Without them, you may never create anything. There are far too many failed artists who never

50. Grant Hilary Brenner, "Your Brain on Creativity," *Psychology Today*, February 22, 2018, https://www.psychologytoday.com/us/blog /experimentations/201802/your-brain-creativity.

even took the first step. With the tenets, though, you can live out your artistic dreams and fulfill them all the way to having a finished product.

Be Authentic

In both magickal practices and the creative arts, authenticity is vital. You must "know thyself" before any magick happens. Your unique interests and expressions should be celebrated. They're part of who you are, and you can use them whenever you create. You may think that some aspects of yourself are too weird or emotional to use in your art, but consider using them anyway. What sets you apart from others could be fundamental to your success.

When I was a beginner fire dancer, I went against what most fire dancers were doing to create my own vision. I combined my love of ballet, costumes, and dramatic music. I made my own fire tools from Kevlar gloves and wire, including fire crowns, fans, a belt, and gloves with flaming fingertips. I played dramatic music that inspired me, and I wore strange costumes that brought the performance to life. These unique expressions of dancing felt true to me, and I showcased them in my monthly fire shows. Because I didn't charge admission for those shows, I had no strict instructions or an investment to show up a certain way. I merely wanted to express what moved me, which would hopefully move someone else. Years later, when I was negotiating top-dollar fire performances almost every weekend, I asked my clients whether they wanted me to use more mainstream fire tools, music, and clothing. I assumed they wanted a toned-down version of my fire dancing—which is what most other people offered. I was surprised when, every single time, none of them wanted me to change a thing. Not a single person. They didn't want to hire a copycat artist. They wanted my unique style because it made me stand out in a sea of other performers.

Trust your authenticity. Trust your unique vision of your art. Even if your creations build upon a concept from another artist, it's likely you'll have a unique take on it. Be yourself, and allow yourself to shine.

Focus on One Project

One of the best things that a beginner artist can do is to choose one project for their focus. It may seem fun to be a jack-of-all-trades, and it's natural to desire a variety of expressions. There's nothing wrong with that approach, but when your focus is diffuse among many projects, it'll limit your ability to go deep into one area. At the end of the day, you probably won't accomplish as much compared to if you had only one project. For example, someone who practices four very different arts, such as dance, painting, writing, and singing, will have four different mental starting points for their arts and four sets of ideas associated with each art. They'll also have one-quarter the amount of free time for each art, and one-quarter of the mental capacity for the insights associated with each discipline.

It's far easier to not juggle several arts at the same time. When you solely focus on one discipline, you'll be led down the path of making your art and refining it to its greatest capacity. This isn't to say that you can't combine arts that are related. This is actually a great way to get ideas for your art. For example, learning four styles of painting or experimenting with four different kinds of paint will allow you to grow your painting skill set and give you variety, which can be used later in your art.

If focusing on one project makes you feel limited, remember that it's a starting point and not something you'll have to stick with forever. It's a guideline and not a strict rule. Sometimes, doing another form of art will give you exercise or relaxation, so it may be worth doing it as long as you can prioritize one art over the other.

Use the Days of the Week for Inspiration

As you begin your project, it's smart to draw upon the energies at hand for an extra boost of magick. One of the best ways to do this is to use the deeper meanings behind the seven days of the week. This cycle has been in place since Sumerian times, and it probably helped ancient people maintain the good working order in their personal lives and in society. Later, the Babylonians dedicated a day to the moon, the sun, and the most visible planets. Due to the vast history of people using these days for specific purposes for millennia, each day has associated energies.

You can tap into these energies in your magickal creative practices by being aware of the energies and calling upon them or setting an intention for use in your art. For example, on Sunday, you could set an intention to do work that lets your spirit shine, and you can designate Wednesday to be the day when you draw upon the commercial energy at hand to take care of your artistic finances. Ideally, this information will inspire you and not make you feel limited to certain activities. It may also be that the best time to create is when you have the time and you feel inspired.

Sunday (Sun): Power, motivation, community, growth, radiance, confidence

Monday (Moon): Magick, dreams, emotions, healing, depths

Tuesday (Mars): Courage, ability, determination, motivation, focus, competition

Wednesday (Mercury): Communication, business, travels, insights, opportunities

Thursday (Jupiter): Expansion, luck, happiness, fortune, abundance, wealth

Friday (Venus): Beauty, attraction, passion, relationships, love

Saturday (Saturn): Completion, structure, learning, time management, discipline

Creative Correspondences for Air: Sounds and Aromas

Inspiration is essential for creativity, and two of the best correspondences for it are sounds and aromas. They support the creative mindset by letting us dial in to the specific energy of our projects. With their influence, we can usher in the creative spirit and receive an influx of ideas.

SOUNDS

Sounds inspire creation. They have the power to shift the energy in your creative space by cleansing it and immersing it in a specific mood. They also have the power to alter your mindset to be more conducive to your art. You may recall from chapter 1 that the Greek root word for *muse* means "song." Songs and soundscapes can give you the key to clarify your ideas and improve them as well. Music inspired Pamela Colman Smith, the occult artist who created the iconic images for the Rider-Waite tarot deck, now called the Rider-Waite-Smith deck. Smith often used music to induce images while she was creating. In an interview about some of her paintings that were inspired by classical music, she said, "[They're] what I see when I hear music—thoughts loosened and set free by the spell of sound. When I take a brush in hand and the music begins, it is like unlocking the door into a beautiful country."[51] This also illustrates the transportive effects of music.

Do any songs inspire you to create? Do any remind you of your art? If so, play them as you create. What about the scenery of your art? If it had a soundtrack or a soundscape, what would it be? If you're a visual artist or a dancer, what music would you choose for your gallery opening or the performance of your dance? If you're a fiction writer, what kind of music would your protagonist listen to as they pursued their goals? Try to find music that puts you in the location of your art. Make a playlist of songs or sounds and play it as you create.

For others who prefer to not listen to music, audiobooks and podcasts have the power to clear away stray thoughts. They encourage artists to relinquish their mental chatter to someone else's flow of energy, which can let the creative spirit in. Often, these artists find that their hands somehow know what to do without giving any conscious thought to their art.

Sounds are a gift to artists. They will let you find the right vibe for your project and shift your mindset into a creative space, both of which attract the creative spirit. Ideally, your sounds will promote a sustaining background vibe that enhances your art and doesn't distract from it. For this reason, writers often prefer music with no words, and physical artists like sculptors, potters, and painters may prefer audiobooks or podcasts. Listen to different kinds of sounds to see what inspires you. You'll know you've

51. George Newnes, ed., "Pictures in Music," *The Strand Magazine*, vol. 35, January–June 1908, 634, https://archive.org/stream/in.ernet.dli .2015.24894/2015.24894.The-Strand-Magazine-1908-Vol35_djvu.txt.

found the right sound when you can dial your energy in to your project and sustain it for a while. For the most immersive results, use headphones. Other artists prefer no sounds at all, and this is also valid. Sound can be a huge distraction. For these people, I recommend wearing earbuds or noise-canceling headphones. These will minimize the distractions happening all around you and let you find your flow.

SOUNDS FOR CREATIVITY

Audiobooks, Fiction: Interesting, evocative, visionary, emotional

Audiobooks, Nonfiction: Intellectual, stimulating, inspiring

Baroque or Classical Music: Intellectual, evocative, refined

Dramatic Music: Emotional, clashing, triumphant, successful, futile

Drumming (Rhythmic): Sustaining, transcendental, spiritual

Major Key Music: Inspiring, emotional, happy, hopeful, simple, evocative of beginnings and endings

Mellow Music: Relaxing, restorative, emotional, easygoing

Minor Key Music: Emotional, brooding, conflicting, struggling, desirous, unfortunate

Podcasts: Interesting, diversity of topics, informative, evocative, stimulating

Soundscapes: Atmospheric, environmental, situational

Trance Music (Droning): Emotional, spiritual, transcendental

Uplifting Music: Upbeat, positive, energetic

AROMAS

When aromas are used in the creative process, they can shift your mindset almost magically. One whiff and you're in a flower garden celebrating a birthday, or you're walking in a peaceful forest. Aromas go directly into our minds, so they bring up memories from the past, which can be used to create. We can also use scents to create new memories. Choose aromas that either inspire you or evoke the essence of your art.

There are many ways to create aromas. One of the easiest ways is to burn incense sticks or to set resin on a lit charcoal disk in a heat-safe vessel such as a cauldron. Another option is to create an essential oil spray bottle with water and essential oils—a general guideline is to use about ten drops of oil for every two ounces of water. You can dilute essential oils in a carrier oil such as almond, coconut, or jojoba, and put it on your wrists or temples—use about five drops of essential oil for every ounce of carrier oil. Another way to enjoy aromas is to aromatize essential oils in a glass vessel that vibrates to spread the scent. If you need a reminder of the cautionary measures to take with essential oils, see chapter 1.

All the aromas in this section are associated with creativity. Their added correspondences are listed. Take note of what works so you can use them again next time.

AROMAS FOR CREATIVITY

Bergamot (*Citrus bergamia*): Focus, calm, inspiration

Copal (*Protium copal*): Cleansing, optimism, mindset

Cypress (*Cupressus*): Focus, steady energy, groundedness

Eucalyptus (*Eucalyptus*): Focus, clarity, enthusiasm, spirit communication

Frankincense (*Boswellia*): Clarity, cleansing, spirit communication

Geranium (*Pelargonium*): Confidence, calm, mindset

Grapefruit (*Citrus ×paradisi*): Confidence, focus, inspiration

Jasmine (*Jasminum*): Self-love, inspiration, confidence, optimism

Lavender (*Lavandula*): Balancing, stimulating, mentally clarifying, expression

Lemon (*Citrus ×limon*): Clarity, focus, optimism, hope

Lilac (*Syringa*): Communication, expression, cleansing

Neroli (*Citrus ×aurantium*): Peace, calm, inspiration, mindset, spirit communication

Orange (*Citrus ×sinensis*): Energy, purification, emotional balance

Peppermint (*Mentha ×piperita*): Focus, spirit communication

Rose (*Rosa*): Self-love, emotional balance, mindset, spirituality

Rosemary (*Salvia rosmarinus*): Memory, concentration

CREATIVE RITUAL: SPIRIT AND AIR

Go to your art workplace and turn off distractions. Organize and tidy up, and then clear your mind. Welcome the creative mindset within and the creative spirit.

Light the incense or use the essential oil. Breathe deeply. Let the aroma inspire you. Play inspiring music or other sounds, and allow your energy to shift to get into the mood of your project. Use your imagination and daydream. Brainstorm to dream up new ideas. Write them down.

• Exercise •
EXPLORING CREATIVE INTENTIONS

Creative intentions define who we are and what we want our art to be. When artists are clear about their purposes, they're more likely to take action and feel good about it. You'll be attracted to do the work because you know what it means to you. Just like magickal intentions, they have to be specific, but not too specific. Answering these questions will be especially helpful for new artists and for anyone who doesn't know what their next project should be. Don't overthink the answers—your first responses are likely the best. It's okay if you don't know the answers to these questions yet—just write what you do know.

PERSONAL STATEMENT

Who are you at your core? What are your strengths? What do you stand for? Write a few words here. When we come from a place of knowing, we can move with more purpose in the world. Here's an example: I am a determined and genuine person and a lover of beauty, nature, magickal practices, and music.

_____

_____

_____

_____

_____

_____

ARTIST INTENTION STATEMENT

What is your intention for being an artist? Why do you want to create? Write down a few reasons that come to mind. If your intentions include selling your art or public recognition, jot down at least two other intentions. These added beliefs will give you a more diverse base for you to gauge your success, which will help you feel more fulfilled about the creative process. Here are some examples: I want to be an artist so I can be in the flow state, to express my emotions, to have fun with my friends, to rebel against something, to create something magickal, to feel a sense of accomplishment, to share my dreams with the world, and so on.

_____

_____

_____

_____

_____

_____

_____

_____

_____

_____

_____

ARTISTIC INTERESTS

What are you generally interested in? What could you spend a lot of time learning about or doing? Write down all kinds of interests, even if they don't seem to have anything to do with creativity. Here's an example: astrology, ritual, graphic design, Ukrainian folklore, ballads, gardening, reading, cooking, travel, etc.

_____

_____

_____

_____

What kind of art inspires you? What moves you? For example, impressionist paintings, modern dance, children's stories, and sculpture.

_____

_____

_____

_____

Has anything sparked your imagination recently? Write down the source and what you imagined.

_____

_____

_____

_____

What artistic media are you most interested in doing? Write down a few. For example, painting, musicals, and woodwork.

_____

_____

_____

_____

Is there any kind of art you always wished was in the world but isn't? What is it?

_____

_____

_____

_____

YOUR CREATIVE PROJECT

Now, let's pair some of your artistic concepts together to create projects for you to consider working on. Combine one of your interests or inspirations with one of your artistic media. These should show you an interesting way to combine what already moves you with your preferred methods of expression. Write down a few ideas. Here are some examples using the previous answers: a musical inspired by Ukrainian folklore, a series of paintings made in the impressionist style series for all the zodiac signs, wood carvings inspired by children's stories, and a modern dance performance inspired by a ritual.

After you've written down a few, figure out which one feels the most attractive to you and draw a star beside it. This will be your project, and you'll explore it further in the rest of this section. If you decide you don't like it, feel free to select another one.

How can you express yourself through your project? What special touches could you use to make it stand out as yours? For example, if you chose paintings of the zodiac signs, you could paint a certain way or use a special color. If you need inspiration, review what you wrote down about your general interests. For example, if your interests include gardening and magick, you could paint images of the corresponding plants as well as magickal symbols, sigils, or colors.

Now, it's time to think big about your project. Let loose your imaginative brain. If the sky was the limit and money was no concern, what would you create? What if your project could defy the laws of nature? Write down your grandest visions. Thinking big expands our minds beyond what we perceive our limitations to be. Some of the ideas you write here may never work, and that's okay. When we have big ideas, the inspiration flows and the next point in the path appears. Another reason to be open to the realm of possibilities is because it opens us up to the otherworld. Whether we achieve that vision or not, it can inspire us and the creative spirit. Here's an example: if your project is the ritualistic modern dance, then your larger-than-life ideas could be having the performance in a park, using a real bonfire, or using wires to make your dancers seem to fly through the air.

• Exercise •
BRAINSTORM YOUR PROJECT

Brainstorming is the next step in the creative process. It's one of the best ways to successfully develop a good idea. I'm always surprised by how easily things come together—connections seem to arise out of nowhere. To try this activity, plan to have private time for about ten to fifteen minutes.

In the center of a blank piece of paper, write the broad vision of your project (from the exercise). Draw a circle around it, and then draw four short spokes coming off the circle.

For each spoke, write down any idea that comes to mind when you think of the broad vision. Expand the vision with the finer details. Write down ideas that go with it, no matter how simple, odd, or impossible they may seem. Don't be afraid to think outside the box.

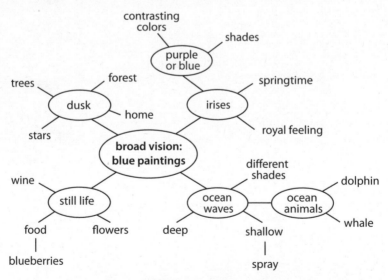

Figure 1: Example of a Brainstorm

If the secondary ideas make you think of anything else, draw a circle around them, add spokes, and write the ideas coming off them. Think big—add whatever seems connected. It's okay to write down ideas that may seem impossible or out of your budget right now. Keep writing ideas until you can't think of anything else. In the next chapter, you'll use this to make a rough outline of your concept.

Tips for Mental Creativity

- Use your imagination and play with your ideas. Have fun!
- Create a story in your mind about your topic. Write down anything interesting.
- Keep track of the songs that get you in the mood for your project by adding them to a special playlist.
- Learn more about your genre and immerse yourself in your creative medium. Ask questions and look up the answers. Fall down a rabbit hole as you follow interesting leads. See your art in its natural setting, if possible. Read books about it, listen to podcasts about it, and watch videos and movies that show your favorite art and the artists who made it. Take it all in and let it inspire you to create. A big part of the beginning phase is getting into the right mindset so you can eventually think about your project in a structured way and set habits. This will all come in the future—for now, simply learn as much as you can.
- Take notes of any artistic ideas that inspire you. It's important to capture them, no matter how ludicrous they may sound at the time. Some of your best ideas will come to you when you're about to sleep or when you're on automatic

mode, such as driving or riding a train. You may think you'll remember them, but often, they disappear without a trace. I suggest using a special notebook to record these notes. You can also use an application on your phone, such as one that takes notes or one that records your voice. Be sure to reference your project title and any other relevant information, especially if you have multiple projects. For example, "Chapter 2 of the tarot book," "idea for a hedgehog painting," or "golden eyeshadow idea for the futuristic show." Every so often, compile all your notes into your notebook so they're all in one place.

In the Air

As you start to think about your creative journey, you may feel that your project is nebulous. It's okay if you feel this way. Continue to believe in yourself and your project. You'll delve deeper into your art, and things will progress. As you go forward, be sure to keep an open mind. The more flexible and open you are with your project, the more your creative spirit can assist you. It's also important to remember that happiness lies along the path of creating *and* in the destination (the final product). All too often, artists sacrifice feelings of happiness while they create because they get fixated on an endpoint. They believe that only when their goals are accomplished can they allow themselves to be happy. This is almost certainly a recipe for disaster. Instead of falling into that mental trap, try to find joy in all aspects of creation. Art absorbs whatever energy we put into it, and feeling constrained can affect the energy of art. Far better is to live your best life possible as you create. You deserve to feel satisfaction and happiness throughout the entirety of your creative journey.

CHAPTER 3

Fire: Passion and Courage

Fire is an important ally in the creative process. When you take the airy visions of your project and add heat and passion, your art transforms. Fire burns the extraneous fluff away. The vision that remains becomes stronger through the process of tempering. You'll be changed by experience with fire as well—it'll show you what you love, ignite your courage to keep going, and set boundaries around whatever doesn't stoke your excitement. This chapter will help you put your art into the fire and brush off the ashes to get a more interesting project, which rouses the creative spirit even more.

Courage

One of the biggest lessons a beginning artist learns is how to have the courage to create. It takes a lot of guts to make art. In a world with so much amazing art, it's not always easy to try new things, but you should try anyway. Think of it this way—we all start somewhere. No one's first attempt at their art was a masterpiece, and that's okay. If you're a perfectionist and a beginner, I'll kindly ask you to lower your expectations. At this point, it's all about expressing yourself and having fun. Always remember that it's okay to be a beginner. It's the only way you'll learn.

> Art is magic:
> It combines your mind,
> imagination, and spirit
> with energy and passion
> in a way that affects you
> and others who view
> or experience it.
>
> —MICHAEL HERKES

After having the courage to try, the next lesson that most artists learn is how to be both authentic and vulnerable at the same time. This is a more advanced lesson, like Courage 2.0. It relies upon a firm foundation of the first lesson (trying new things). To succeed at this goal, we have to know who we are and be transparent about that in our art. We need to seek that level of expression even if we never show our creations to anyone else. Dave Grohl, the founder of the Foo Fighters and the drummer for Nirvana, believes this quality is essential. He writes, "Courage is the defining factor in the life of any artist. The courage to bear your innermost feelings, reveal your true voice.…It's the courage to be yourself that bridges…opposing emotions, and when it does, magic can happen."[52] It may seem strange to hold such different emotions within us, but everyone has courage and fear within them. It's completely natural too, as opposite parts of a whole are found in nature. Consider magnets. They have two poles—a negative and a positive—and yet they're both on the same piece of metal. Like magnets, we can find a happy medium and express our vulnerable, complicated selves with a steady hand. We can dance with our fears, sing a sad song with a brave voice, and write a love story during loss. We contain multitudes, and the best art does too because it reflects that.

52. Dave Grohl, *The Storyteller: Tales of Life and Music* (New York: William Morrow, 2021), 355.

The challenge to be a courageous artist will come up again and again, especially when you share your work. There's more about that in part 2. For now, just know that it really is magickal to work with your visions and put yourself out there.

Activating Your Creative Potential

Creative potential is like a book of matches. You can have it, but if you never start a fire, you'll never know how much light you can create. Everyone has the potential to do creative work, but most people don't take this important step on the artist's journey and actually light it up. I write about this from personal experience. For years, passive tendencies plagued me. It's pretty common, especially if the world puts you in second place (or third, or fourth, or last). Without knowing it, I absorbed the message that I was not an artist, even though I wanted to be. And so, for years, I only ever used my creative potential to light other people's fires. Sure, I had visions of what I could make, but I didn't know how to start. The next step—trying my hand at art—seemed too enormous and intimidating. More than anything, I wished that a benevolent stranger would see my artistic potential and swoop me up into another life where they'd give me all the training and resources I needed. Sadly, this wishful thinking was the only way that I felt I could activate my creative potential.

After several years of these feelings, I knew I had to change. Instead of waiting for someone else to be my hero, I decided to become the person I was looking for. I would see the artistic potential within myself. I would give myself everything I needed to create. It took a lot of courage and course-corrections, but I was determined to try. My dreams were too important to give up on. I didn't want to make it to the end of my life and have regrets about letting other people's opinions stop me from ever trying. As a result of this mental shift, I started showing up for myself and my artistic visions. This is when something magickal happened—it was as if my heart ignited, and the fire sustained me so I could keep going. Shortly afterward, the creative spirit came to me.

If any part of this story resonates with you, please use it as fuel. Ignite your creative potential the same way I did. Don't use your creative fires to make escapist fantasies like the little match girl. Be your own hero. Save yourself from wondering "what if?"

Chapter 1 says that the first step on the artist's journey is to get an artist's mindset. Artists need to believe they are artists and that they can create art. The next step is to be brave and passionate about your art—so much so that it ignites your potential, you test those beliefs, and you try.

Please light your own fires. I can tell you from experience that it's worth it.

Find the Passion

Passion is a huge driver of creativity. Think of a time in your life when you felt like you were lit up like a bonfire. You may have felt an intense longing, sparkling excitement, or hot lust. You may have burned with a feverish love or a zealous enthusiasm. Passion feels like fire. Like a magnet, it guides us toward what we desire the most. Every artist feels passion for their work. While you could do creative work that doesn't make you feel like a firecracker exploding in the sky, would you want to? Passion will keep you coming back to your art for more. Here are some hot tips on feeling the heat.

FOCUS ON WHAT YOU LOVE

If you ever used a magnifying glass to focus the sun's rays onto something combustible, you know it can make fire. Similarly, when you focus on what you love about your project, you can start a fire that will keep you feeling excited about the creation process. In the last chapter, you used the element of air to dream big, and you searched for all kinds of fantastic thoughts. Even though you identified those ideas, it doesn't mean you must use them in your art. It's okay if some of your ideas don't continue forward from the air chapter. It's best to focus on the ones that draw you in the most—the ones that make you feel alive and electric. The creative spirit likes ideas, but it really loves love. If your heart isn't in it, it'll leave.

Unfortunately, a lot of artists often talk themselves out of making what they love. They think their ideas are too weird and no one else would appreciate them. They believe their art isn't popular enough to market. They think someone else has already done it, so they shouldn't even try. They tell themselves all kinds of stories that basically amount to "no one will love this, it's too weird, and it won't be good enough." This is the killing fire talking—the kind that burns everything and never gives anything a chance to live. It's not useful, and it's not true either. With eight billion people on the planet, there's a good chance that a lot of people would appreciate their art. Most people can feel when something comes from the heart, and in accordance with the law of correspondences, they often react similarly to it. Trust that you can make art that makes you happy.

BE REBELLIOUS

Just as you can feel passion toward something you love, you can also feel passionate about something you loathe or disagree with.

When you rebel against something, you can use its power against itself. Is there something you have a strong opinion about or which makes you angry? Do you want to be a voice for an under-represented group to which you belong? Is there something you'd like to respond to? Use your art to talk back. There's something so fiery about being in retaliation. Use your fireball reactions in your art. Allow them to propel you forward. Even if your project never gets you revenge or payback, it can still be the fire under your butt that keeps you creating.

USE COMPETITION AS FRICTION

A little competition can fan the flames of your creativity. One of the best ways to inspire passion is to compete with yourself. There are so many ways to take advantage of this. For instance, you could try to create for more hours than you did the previous week, or you could try to finish your art faster than the last time. You could try for a more elaborate design or for an award. If you can turn these fiery feelings into a game, they'll blast your project forward. You only have a chance of winning this competition if you stay in the race. In other words, keep creating.

You can also compete with your friends or rivals if you keep it amicable. Consider setting up a contest or a bet about who can finish their project first, produce more, or win an award. This can make you start creating, and it can keep going when you thought you'd quit. You may find yourself finishing your project early and creating more often so you'll beat your rival. If you use competition to inspire passion, be sure to keep it light. Don't let it ruin a friendship. Our peers are often our greatest friends and supporters. Remember to feel happy for their successes too. When you don't win a competition, take it in stride. The real purpose is to enter the race and try your best. If it inspired any creativity, you won too.

Envious feelings can act as a kind of friction to propel you to create. Jealousy is often a sign that you desire something for yourself, and if they have done it, that means you could too. A healthy dose of jealousy can inspire creation, but an unhealthy amount can create feelings of stress and unworthiness. If you ever feel less than your rival or obsessed with measuring progress, take a break from competition to reorganize your thoughts and do shadow work. Make sure you're not too hard on yourself. Envy is only useful to us as creative friction when it inspires us, not when it blocks us. If this course of action isn't helping you succeed, evaluate another path of inspiration.

Use the Ticking Clock

Even though it's a cliché to race against the clock, it's still around in movies and other media because it works. There's something hugely motivational about a ticking clock that incites action. This is often because there's a set time when the clock will stop and your time to do the creative work will be over. Deadlines are one of the most commonly used types of ticking clocks. Knowing that someone is counting on you to produce something by a certain date can light a fire under you unlike anything else. If no one sets a deadline for your progress, set one for yourself—choose a date and a realistic goal. Write it down on your calendar and backtrack your time to figure out how much you have to do every day or week.

You may also feel the ticking clock when there's a window of opportunity that you must use or lose. For instance, if you'll have two months of time with only a few responsibilities, you could try your hand at an art project. You can be motivated by your age. If you've always wanted to write a book before you turned fifty, and you're currently forty-seven years old, you could feel pressure to start writing. People often want to be the first one with the idea or to present something before anyone else lays claim to it.

A ticking clock should feel like a good kind of pressure to do your creative work, like a game or an exciting adventure. It's important to realize if it ever feels harmful. It's never a good idea to sacrifice everything for your art. If you find yourself stressed by the ticking clock, you may need to give yourself more compassion and an extension. Be sure to give yourself a break between "ticking clock" projects too. Stress blocks creativity, so if you ever feel overwhelmed by a deadline, it may not be as helpful as you think. Remember, moderation is good for creativity.

Boundaries

Like a wall of flames, a boundary draws a line between you and anything you don't want. No one wants to cross through a wall of flames, and that's how our limits should be too. When you enforce your boundaries as if they are walls of fire that can't be crossed, you can become much more successful. This section evaluates where you're spending your most precious creative currency—time. We only have so many hours in one day and only so much creative time within those hours. Thinking like a CEO will give you more time, direction, and success.

OTHER CREATIVE OUTLETS

Many people use a lot of their creative energy during their free time, but they don't realize it. Creativity is used in all kinds of normal activities, like baking and tidying the home. People tap into creative ideas when they wear fashionable clothing and groom themselves with makeup and hairstyles. They make creative decisions whenever they take photos, edit them, and write a few lines for social media. No one has an infinite amount of creative energy. All this thinking, planning, generating ideas, and making decisions can steal valuable time away from your project.

If these activities fulfill you creatively, by all means, keep them. Keep whatever makes you happy and gives you the most diverse experiences. For instance, if one of your creative tasks involves friends, and you would be lonely otherwise, think about keeping it. A balanced life is always best to maintain creative energy. Figure out how to balance the time you spend on them with the time you'll spend on your project. If those outlets don't spark joy, cut back on them, especially if you're more passionate about your art. It'll give you a lot more time, which will further your project along.

ENDLESS TASKS

There are so many tasks that have nothing to do with creativity, like work, checking emails, paying bills, taking care of family, scrolling through social media, cleaning, listening to podcasts, and other entertainment. Just thinking about all these things can extinguish the match of creative potential before it's even lit. Some of these tasks are necessary, and they must be kept. By all means, go to work, take care of your family, and pay the bills. Take a moment to consider if you're doing extra work, though. If your child is older and they don't need as much one-on-one time, take the opportunity to cut back a little so you can have more time to create. If you don't have to stay at work late or go to the grocery store, don't do it. Anything that's not urgent or necessary can be cut back or bound. For the non-urgent tasks, like checking social media, responding to emails, and doing chores, you could make a rule to only engage in them on one or two days per week. For example, on Sunday mornings, after you've had two cups of coffee, you'll go through all the emails you received that week, as well as your social media notifications. It's much easier to identify spam and items that don't require a response if you do it less often. If you had checked your email and gone on social media several times each day, this practice could save you an hour or more every week.

Another example of a boundary with endless tasks is to only do optional things after you've done all the necessary things. For instance, you can listen to podcasts or watch television only after you've done your creative work and taken care of your family. Little changes like these can free up a lot of time and energy.

THE CHILLER

There may come a time when you feel the passion raging within you, and you're ready to create. And then, someone comes along and blows out your flame. In gambling, there's a term for someone who makes a table go cold—"the chiller." The winning streaks end and everyone loses money. This happens with creative energy too. It could be a person, a pet, some tedious action, someone on social media or social media itself, the news, or an idea. Any of these things has the potential to blow out your fire and chill your creativity.

Sometimes, it comes from those we love. For instance, your friend or partner may want to interact at an inopportune time, or you could have a pet who wants attention. They likely don't snuff your fire on purpose, but you do need to set boundaries with them. To keep your fire going, remove yourself from their presence while you're working. Make a sign that says, "I'm creating now, so don't bother me unless there's a real emergency." Go into another room and close the door. Go away from the people and do your art somewhere else, like a studio or a library. You could also make a rule that if you're wearing a special piece of clothing such as a painter's smock, it means don't interact with you. Don't be afraid of limits. Like some fires, boundaries are necessary for new life to begin.

• Exercise •
EXPLORING BOUNDARIES

Take about thirty minutes for this exercise. Do the creative ritual and answer these questions.

Who supports your art? Who cheers you on as you talk about what you want to create?

_____

_____

_____

_____

Who has said negative things about your art?

_____

_____

_____

_____

As a creator, you have an active role in defining your world. What responsibilities are absolutely necessary for you to keep? For instance, my family, pet obligations, etc.

_____

_____

_____

_____

What can you cut back on, timewise?

_____

_____

_____

_____

Where can you place firmer boundaries? Who or what needs a limit?

_____

_____

_____

_____

What can you delegate to someone else?

_____

_____

_____

_____

What or who can you minimize or cut out of your life?

_____

_____

_____

_____

• *Spell* •
THE "NO" SPELL

We established that you have a limited amount of free time, and it's very precious. This spell is useful to evaluate your options and succinctly say no. It helps you practice saying no without explanations, reasoning, justifications, or other plans—simply because no is your answer. Plan for about ten minutes of alone time when you feel safe, secure, and in touch with yourself. You'll be burning small pieces of paper, so you may want to do this outside.

Materials
birthday candle
heat-safe container such as a medium-size cauldron or a large
    bowl made of ceramic or metal
matches
piece of paper
pencil
scissors

Set up for the spell by placing the candle in the cauldron. The easiest way to do this is to light the candle, drop hot wax into the cauldron or plate, blow the candle out, and affix it to the cauldron with the hot wax.

Write down all your options for tasks you could accomplish, either for the time remaining in the current day or for tomorrow. Your activities could include things like exploring your creative project, doing a favor for a stranger just because they asked, going on social media, washing the bedding, baking cookies for the school fundraiser, procrastinating, resting, reading a book, and exercising. Cut these options into little pieces of paper.

Next, hold the book of matches and feel the creative potential within you. Consider what you could do with your limited amount of free time. Strike a match. Gaze at the dazzling light for a second, and then light the birthday candle. This tiny candle represents your limited creative energy and the decisions you must make on the fly.

Read your options, one by one, aloud. Connect with your body and how that option makes you feel. If anything does not spark joy within you from the first moment, say no firmly, light the piece of paper on fire, and drop it into the cauldron. You have a limited amount of time, so go with your gut. When you have burned all the options that don't excite you, blow out the candle. Leave it sitting there until the next day to remind you of everything you don't want to do. Place the remaining scraps of paper in your pocket and do the things you want to do. Follow up with communication to the appropriate people about your boundaries.

This spell can also be used to burn away unhelpful thoughts or influences. Simply replace the list of activities with thoughts or influences, and burn the ones that aren't helpful.

Creative Correspondences for Fire: Ignition and Candles

Lighting a candle is a sacred act. When you think about everything our ancestors did to start fires and maintain them, you can see how wonderful our modern tools are. I imagine that our ancestors love modern-day candles, lighters, and matches because they may not have had items as nice or effective as ours.

When you strike a match of your creative potential, the flames are bright, attractive, and mesmerizing. It's sort of like falling in love and feeling the passionate burn of having a crush in your heart. However, no match can sustain a flame for long. It must be transferred to a place where it can be supported—a candle. With their reservoirs of fuel, candles are like solid, lasting relationships with your creative potential. They'll take the light and keep it burning throughout the long nights. Both aspects are part of the creative ritual for fire. A lit candle represents your passion, determination, courage, creativity, willpower, and ability to engage in transformation.

Fire safety is always important. Place extinguished matches and lit candles on heat-safe surfaces. Position your candles so they're far away from anything overhead or nearby. Never leave a candle unattended, and make sure your candles are completely out before leaving the room.

IGNITION

Matches and lighters are important aspects of any magick that involves a flame, but their corresponding energies are often overlooked. I believe they carry specific energies just as much as a candle. Because your fire starter will be used as part of your ritual, use something that makes you feel passionate. That makes it easier for you to see the fiery energy mirrored within you in the flame more easily. Decorate the outside of your ignition tool with colors, words, or images that make you feel excited about your project.

IGNITION SOURCES

Lighter (Brass): Protection, strength, resourcefulness, communication

Lighter, Long-Necked (Plastic and Brass): Versatility, elegance, strength, protection

Lighter, Short (Plastic): Utility, universal, ease

Matches, Book (Cardboard): Utility, durability, flexibility, versatility

Matches, Long (Wood, Usually White Pine or Aspen): Longevity, magick, elegance, protection, spirit communication

Matches, Short (Wood, Usually White Pine or Aspen): Strength, balance, protection, spirit communication

CANDLES

Nearly any candle can be used for your creative project, but some candles are better than others because of their color, size, or shape. These things matter to magicians because of the law of correspondences. Physical objects represent different things in a purely energetic aspect. For example, a two-inch birthday candle has a vastly different energy compared to a seven-day candle encased in glass, and that's different from a five-inch candle in the shape of a woman or a goddess.

To take advantage of the creative ritual, choose candle shapes with burn times that match the length of your sessions. For example, if you create for long sessions, such as three hours at a time, use a candle that lasts longer than a tealight, which often doesn't last longer than two hours. The longer session time ensures that by the time you blow your candle out, there will be an even melt across their top, which is one of the secrets to prolonging the life of a big candle. Conversely, if you create for short periods, say thirty minutes at a time, your best choices will be taper candles or tealight candles. They can be blown out without concern for the melting wax, and you can feel a sense of accomplishment with the change produced in them.

Of course, you can light more than one candle. Burn two or more candles to stoke extra excitement about your project. If you can't have an open flame, use an LED candle. Just be sure to have spare batteries on hand in case you need them.

CANDLE TYPES

Chime: Utility, flow, long or short sessions

LED: Versatility, safety, consistency, good for long or short sessions

Pillar: Accomplishment, success, vision, flow, long sessions

Pillar Enclosed in Glass: Safety, elegance, duration, long sessions

Seven-Day Candle Enclosed in Glass: Safety, elegance, purpose, perseverance, long sessions

Shaped Candles: Specific purposes, extra magick, flow, long sessions

Taper, Dipped: Elegance, steadiness, depth, flow, long and short sessions

Taper, Poured: Elegance, utility, flow, long and short sessions

Tea Light: Baby steps, progress, new artists, new projects, short sessions

Votive: Flow, balance, medium to long sessions

CANDLE COLORS

Colors have traditional and individual meanings, and we have feelings about them. When it comes to choosing colors for our projects, we can go about it two different ways. The first is to think about your project and what color comes up the most. If your character faces slate-gray rain every day, this color could be used as an inspiration for you to keep that energy going throughout the novel as a theme. The second way to use candle color is to choose one that makes you feel inspired to do your creative work. For instance, maybe a bright, sunshine-yellow candle will help you feel lit up from within, especially if you write about a rainy world.

It's important to use a color that you have feelings about because this can increase your energy. Sometimes, it can come down to the preferences between not only colors but also shades, or that color across a light and dark spectrum. Consider the difference between different shades of the same color: pink, magenta, mauve, scarlet, crimson red, garnet, wine, and mahogany. Each of these carries the meaning of a red candle (creativity, action, passion, strength, courage, and willpower). However, they likely evoke different feelings within you. Only you can decide which candles are the best ones for your projects. If you're not sure, try different colors to see what works best. You can always use the candles for other purposes if they're not a good fit for your art.

Colors

Red: Creativity, action, passion, strength, courage, willpower

Orange: Creativity, beginnings, memory, communication, action, intelligence, power

Yellow: Creativity, focus, communication, memory, action, clarity, imagination, learning, willpower

Green: Creativity, courage, grounding, growth

Blue: Communication, clarity, vision, intelligence

Purple: Spirit communication, inspiration, intelligence, power, vision

Black: Spirit communication, beginnings and endings, protection, strength, power, boundaries

Brown: Spirit communication, balance, grounding, courage, focus, healing, stability

Gray: Spirit communication, vision, imagination, learning

White: Creativity, spirit communication, inspiration, willpower, clarity, vision, beginnings

Copper: Energy, growth toward goals, versatility

Gold: Creativity, confidence, awareness, power

Silver: Creativity, spirit communication, inspiration, communication, awareness, clarity

CREATIVE RITUAL:
SPIRIT, AIR, AND FIRE

Go to your art workplace and minimize distractions. Organize and tidy up, and then clear your mind. Welcome the creative mindset within and the creative spirit.

Light the incense or use the essential oil. Let the aroma inspire you. Play inspiring music or other sounds and allow your energy to shift to get into the mood of your project. Review your brainstorm sheet from the previous chapter as well as any notes you've taken recently.

Set up your candle in a safe place. Hold your source of ignition in your hands and find your courage. Feel the creative potential within you. When you are ready to activate it, light it up. Enjoy the light of the flame for a moment, then transfer it to the candlewick. See the flickering flame as a mirror for your inner creative drive and passion. You both showed up to this moment.

• Exercise •
REFINE YOUR BRAINSTORM

Some of the work in this chapter is about refining the myriad of ideas in our brainstorm. This exercise should help you burn away whatever doesn't leave you feeling excited. You'll need about ten minutes. Gather your brainstorm, another blank page, and a highlighter or marker in a fiery color, if possible. Get in touch with your passionate feelings by connecting with your heart. On a biological level, you know what rouses you and what doesn't. Think about what you love about your genre of art and what excites you about it. When you are firmly in that emotion, uncap the highlighter or marker and review the brainstorm. Circle the ideas you love the most. Cross out the ideas for which you do not feel any passion. For the neutral ideas, leave them as they are.

Get the clean sheet of paper out. Write down the circled words. Include the neutral words if it feels right. If your art has a natural order to it, write the words in an order that makes sense, such as a beginning, a middle, and an end. Fiction writers may place their favorite things along a plot arc. Painters might work with the location of paintings in a gallery so their ideas flow. It's okay if you don't have any organization. In that case, try using the themes of your art. Keep the brainstorm in a safe place just in case you want to refer to it later.

TIPS FOR PASSIONATE CREATIVITY

- Don't be afraid to follow your strange, attractive dreams.

- Get enthusiastic about your work. The word *enthusiastic* comes from the Greek word *enthousiazein,* which translates to "be possessed or inspired by a god."[53] Having enthusiasm for your art attracts the creative spirit to you.

- Life gives us many busy times, but the "too busy" life is sometimes used as an excuse. Evaluate if that's true for you and if you might be able to carve out time for your dreams. Even if you have to take baby steps toward your goals, you'll make progress.

- Continue to research what you love and take notes.

Up in Flames

If you have the slightest inclination to make art at this point in your life, I encourage you to do so. The first time you light up your creative potential, you'll find a source of light and heat so great that it transforms you. Let it burn away your doubts and worries, as well as overthinking. Keep your fire stoked—it'll come in handy as we make progress on the art.

---

53. Online Etymology Dictionary, s.v. "enthusiastic (*adj.*)," accessed October 12, 2022, https://www.etymonline.com/word/enthusiastic.

CHAPTER 4

Water: Balance and Flow

Art and emotion are intrinsically linked. Creating can calm a stormy mind and soothe troubled emotions. It can also foster feelings of joy and accomplishment. There's a reflexive side to this as well. When we incorporate emotions into our art, we can express the mysterious feelings within and know ourselves better. This starts a deep healing process that unfolds the more we create.

In magickal literature and myth, water is associated with emotions and healing. It also corresponds with creativity and the creative flow. This is the feeling or state we experience when the creative spirit inspires us with energy and ideas. This chapter encourages a healthy flow of creativity and emotions to go deeper into ourselves and our art.

Creativity and Emotions

Children are naturally creative. They invent stories, bring characters to life, and make art with vibrant playfulness. When you were a child, you were probably the same way. Many of us recall when this surface-level part of ourselves sank into the deep sea of emotion. Sometime around grade school, we engage in interpersonal relationships and encounter judgment. The creative inclination retreats even deeper into the sea around puberty when we develop relationships within larger networks that show us impossible standards. Comparison, judgment, and traumas all shut down self-expression. It's a protective mechanism to fit in and survive.

Even when we've outgrown some of the repressive relationships and we're no longer in trauma, many people remain in a shut-down emotional space. They feel too afraid to create, lest their childhood bully appear from the shadows of their minds to say something mean. The natural artist isn't gone. Not at all. It still lives within us, but we must nurture that part of ourselves so we can move through the emotional blocks that hold us back. Clarissa Pinkola Estés compares creativity to a river which can be damaged by harsh conditions: "To bring back the creative life, the waters have to be made clean and clear again. We have to wade into the sludge, purify the contaminants, reopen the apertures, [and] protect the flow from future harm."[54] In other words, we must get dirty and do a little work. We all have our own contamination and blocks. The good news is you don't have to wait to be whole before you create, and you have the power to change this through art.

You Can Create

All the books about creativity have the same message: anyone can create. It's a natural human ability. There are a couple of ways of looking at creative talent. One is the perfectionist model, in which you believe artists have natural talent, and they were born knowing how to paint portraits. With this way of thinking, you either have talent, or you don't, and anyone who doesn't produce museum-level work on their first try will be talentless forever.

54. Estés, *Women Who Run With the Wolves*, 300.

The other way of looking at talent is the progress model, in which some people have a modicum of natural talent or beneficial factors, but more than anything else, hard work is the determining factor in their abilities. Some natural talent is genetic: for instance, some people's bone structure is perfect for ballet. Other aspects are circumstantial, like being born at the right place and time, which can give you the resources you need when a window of opportunity is open. However, neither of these factors guarantees greatness without the work. We can't control the genes we inherited or our upbringing, so it's best to not be concerned about them. We can control how much passion and how many hours we put into our art. If you're concerned that your art won't be perfect on the first try, release the perfectionism model and step into the progress model. First attempts are rarely masterpieces, but you will improve with practice. Everyone does.

Another belief that holds people back from creating is the importance of degrees and official training. Just as you don't need to be initiated in a tradition to be a magickal practitioner or a witch, you don't have to attend art schools to be an artist. All paths to art are valid. The self-trained creator who learns by reading a vast quantity of books, listening to podcasts, watching videos, and discussing ideas and concepts with other artists is just as valid. You don't have to go to school to be good. You just need dedication.

CATHARTIC ART

Have you ever been moved by a work of art? If so, it's likely the artist used their feelings in their creative work. When this happens, the result is often palpable and transcendent. Viewing an artist's healing journey expressed through their art can create a ripple effect of healing within everyone else who partakes of the art. This is a magickal aspect of art that is often overlooked.

It turns out that this kind of creativity is really good for artists' mental health. It gives us the ability to express emotions that are difficult to explain. It allows us to externalize our feelings and put them into a context that makes sense for us. By defining our emotional responses, we have greater control over them. When artists use negative emotions in their art, it often gives greater objectivity over the distress and separation from it. This reduces stress and promotes a feeling of clarity. When artists express positive emotions in art, they can feel a greater sense of integrity, hope, and self-actualization. All kinds of other emotions can be used in art as well. Emotions will likely come up during the creation process. Consider putting them into your art.

• Exercise •
ART AS THERAPY

When we express our inner conflicts through art, we can recreate how we view them and recover the lost parts of ourselves.[55] Grab a large piece of paper and a crayon—these materials evoke childhood for many people. You can use your other artist's tools if you prefer.

Draw a picture of yourself in a moment when someone shut down your creative spirit, but instead of being true to what happened, reframe it. Show yourself as creative and magickal—how you were before that person said or did something mean. If you want, you can draw that person apologizing, or you could show yourself not believing them or not listening. As you draw, feel

---

55. Malchiodi, *Art Therapy Sourcebook*, 36.

the emotion of standing in your strength. Use this drawing art to give yourself the energy they tried to steal. In many ways, this art isn't a lie. There's still some part of you that's creative that no one could ever diminish. That's what we're showing.

Feel free to draw any images that come to mind, as well as thought bubbles, words, symbols, and other people. Don't worry about making your drawing good. It's more about creating it rather than depicting it accurately. No one else will see this unless you want to show them. Add any magickal or mystical details to get the right feeling.

When you're done, give the drawing an empowering title, such as "The Day My Bully Apologized," "How I Learned to Trust My Magick," or "The Voices of Haters Never Reach My Ears."

Take a few deep breaths and say hello to your inner creative self. Welcome them back to your consciousness and tell them you'll protect them from anyone whoever tries to harm them again. Say you hope they feel safe enough to stay with you for all times. If you wish, you can converse about your creative ideas. When you're ready to shift your consciousness back to the world, thank your inner creative self and give yourself a big hug. Exhale deeply and release any energy you moved during the exercise. Run your hands over your body and stretch. When you go about your day, glance in the mirror. You may just see a new sparkle in your eyes.

The Flow State

A lot of artists talk about being in the flow. I believe it happens when our creative spirits give us an abundance of energy to make art. The creative flow is generally described as a heightened, trancelike state in which we feel deeply engrossed in creating.

It can feel different for everyone. Some people describe it as if a switch has been turned on or a current of electricity is running through them. Other people say it's a transcendent feeling that flows through you and into your art, like an overflowing vessel of energy. It has been described as similar to the sensations of falling in love, with an all-consuming excitement and attraction. More than any other element, it seems that watery descriptors are used, including liquid, fluid, stream, river, and drink. I perceive it as a tingly liquid flowing onto my head when I write. When I dance, it feels different. It strikes me in the heart and radiates energy out, directing my limbs with a fluid gracefulness. The flow state often feels magickal and liminal, as if I'm between the worlds. There's nothing like it except for magick and a few other heightened experiences.

THE KNOWING

When I'm in the flow, I have more information. It gives me what I need to make progress on my project at that time. Creating feels easier. It's as if a stream of thoughts flows into me without any effort on my part. All I have to do is accept the flow and let it move through me. The quality of my work is better too. I often find more descriptive words and expressions than the ones I would have thought of on my own. I feel a greater sense of certainty about my art. When I accept the input from the flow, I know deep in my bones that they are the right words or dances. Sometimes, I feel that entire phrases or expressions are perfect as they are, and they won't be changed. There's also a sense that someone else will read them just as they are, and they'll be moved by them. This last feeling is rare but undeniable, as if I'm seeing it from the creative spirit's viewpoint. These are a few examples of the magick of creativity at its finest, and it's how you know the creative spirit is inspiring you.

Being in the flow can feel like you're drinking from a fire hose. The amount of inspiration you receive may be exponentially more than you can possibly use. Try anyway. When it appears, you might be surprised by what happens—your original ideas may pale in comparison to what you actually create. Many fiction writers say that once they got in the flow, their characters came to life with so much personality that they nearly leapt off the screen. When this happens, I let it flow.

INITIATION OF THE FLOW STATE

I believe the creative spirit directs the flow state: they decide who receives it, when it begins, and how long it lasts. Artists can merely create the right conditions for it to occur. As someone who has studied energy, trance, and spirits for many years, I'm aware of the difference between the trance states I produce and those incited by something else. My experiences with the creative spirit are strikingly similar to the encounters I've had with deities and powerful spirits who initiated powerful trances. The consciousness changes are nearly instant, and I can sense the presence of something much greater than myself radiating energy. A sense of awe and stillness comes over me. I'm aware of the option to shut it down and return to my normal life, but I never do as long as the deity or spirit feels benevolent. Their energy feels attractive, and I'm magnetically drawn toward them. I consciously surrender some part of myself so I can interact with them even more. The physical sensations grow stronger, though it's never more than I can handle. Often, the deity or spirit gives me information that I understand despite the lack of words.

There are a few differences between a trance brought on by the creative spirit and one caused by a deity or another powerful entity. With the creative spirit, there are far fewer direct interactions—it's more impersonal, and the main focus is on creative work. The only information I receive is about my project, never about myself. Unlike the powerful entities, the creative spirit isn't directly before me. Rather, it's diagonal—to the side and behind me. I've never felt attracted to my creative spirit, but I do become engrossed in the work. The trance state it incites is slightly more gradual—about ten seconds as opposed to the instantaneous trance brought on by deities and other powerful spirits. Although the amount of time is a little longer, it's still much faster than what I could bring about by myself. The last difference I experience is that the creative flow can last for several hours, which is longer than the majority of interactions I've had with spirits, which ranged from a few seconds to a few hours.

My first interactions with the creative spirit didn't happen until I had put several hours into my project. It also only happened after forming a structure, theme, or outline for my project. It's possible the experience and the structure primed my mind for attracting the creative spirit—this is why the first chapters of this book included that kind of material.

Bring It On

To bring about the creative flow, get out of your head. Tune in to your project's energy instead. Approach the flow state as a magickal experiment. If you don't feel the flow with the correspondences you're using, make changes and see what works. Dig into your niche. When you feel the flow sensations, stay focused on your project and go along with the ideas. Don't try to control it or assert dominance. That will make it dissipate like fog in sunlight. Instead, go where it takes you. Continue to create with those concepts it gives you. Even if an idea has to be scrapped later, it's a good practice to get into the creative flow whenever possible. I advise creating until the spirit's energy stills—until you

Magic is art, and that art— whether that be music, writing, sculpture, or any other form— is literally magic.

—ALAN MOORE

can't hear it anymore. Don't worry about creating anything for the spirit. Create something attractive to you, and the spirit will come.

The amount of time the flow happens is variable. Sometimes it lasts for five seconds and other times five minutes or five hours. It often depends on how many distractions there are and how long you can maintain the flow, physically and mentally. It seems to get stronger and last longer the more it's used, much like a muscle or a neural pathway (or set of pathways). When the flow leaves, give thanks to your creative spirit, stretch, and take a break.

Creative Correspondences for Water: Beverages and Vessels

Beverages do more than just hydrate us. They sustain our energy so we can experience the creative flow. In many ways, water is symbolic of the creative spirit. The muses were associated with several different springs. Drinking from one of the springs even bestowed the gift of poetry. Whenever we drink, we literally replenish our flow. When we see this normal activity as a magickal practice, it can shift our awareness into the creative realm.

BEVERAGES

There's a ritualistic aspect to the steps of making tea. Whenever I select a mug, pour the water into the kettle, choose a tea, boil the water, and pour the hot water over the tea, I feel the creativity flow begin. Perhaps it's because I've done it so many times, or maybe I just have my creative correspondences figured out. My experience with tea inspired the correspondences for this element: cups and beverages.

There are all kinds of beverages you can drink while you create. Ideally, yours should balance your emotions and make you look forward to creating. As you prepare your beverage, slow down your movements to become more aware of the natural flow of energy. Once your beverage is in the mug or cup, hold it in your hands and infuse it with the intention to be in the creative flow. I recommend taking water and another beverage to your creative workspace to balance the effects of the other beverage and stay hydrated.

A few notes of caution: Beware of consuming too much sugar or caffeine. A moderate dose is always better than feeling jittery. Similarly, a small amount of alcohol may be useful for some artists, but for many others, it's detrimental. The quote "Write drunk, edit sober," often attributed to Earnest Hemingway, romanticized alcohol use for creativity. However, there's no citation for it, and other accounts indicate he advocated for sober writing.[56] When drinking alcohol for your art, use restraint, know when you've had more than what's helpful, and when in

---

56. Jess Zafarris, "Did Hemingway Say 'Write Drunk, Edit Sober'? Nope—He Preferred to Write Sober," Writer's Digest, December 20, 2018, https://www.writersdigest.com/be-inspired/did-hemingway-say-write-drunk-edit-sober-nope-he-preferred-to-write-sober.

doubt, take a break. Definitely don't make big changes to your art when you've been drinking. Brewing herbs into a tea also warrants a bit of caution. You'll need to make sure what you brew is safe to consume—don't harvest just anything from anywhere. Start with herbs from the tea section at your grocery. When you brew herbs for the first time, use them sparingly until you're sure you're not allergic. You may also need to do more research and speak with your health care provider if you take medication or if you may be pregnant.

BEVERAGES FOR CREATIVITY

Alcohol: Inspiration, lowered inhibitions, altered focus and mental state

Black Tea: Stimulation, focus, courage, mental power, reflection

Chai Tea: Confidence, strength, stimulation, magick, passion, protection, focus

Coffee: Power, stimulation, focus, sustained energy, awareness

Energy Drinks: Mental power, passion, stimulation, focus

Green Tea: Stimulation, focus, inspiration, mental power, spirituality

Herbal Tea:

- **Ginkgo Leaf (*Ginkgo biloba*):** Mental stimulation, memory, clarity
- **Ginger Root (*Zingiber officinale*):** Confidence, passion, sensuality
- **Hibiscus Flower (*Hibiscus*):** Balance, clarity, insights, calming, spirit
- **Lemon Balm Leaf (*Melissa officinalis*):** Mental clarity, balance, calming

- **Lemon Peel (*Citrus ×limon*):** Clarity, cleansing, insights
- **Licorice Root (*Glycyrrhiza glabra*):** Expression, voice, passion, spirit
- **Mint Leaf (*Mentha*):** Focus, spirit communication, activation, energy
- **Passionflower (*Passiflora*):** Inspiration, calming, flowing
- **Turmeric Root (*Curcuma longa*):** Inspiration, focus, groundedness

Juice: Courage, energy, tenacity, joy, childlike energy

Lemon Water: Cleansing, refreshing, clarity, insights

Rooibos Tea/Red Tea (*Aspalathus linearis*): Courage, tenacity, patience

Water: Cleansing, balancing, refreshing, hydrating, creative flow, healing

VESSELS

You might think that the container for your beverage isn't important, but I believe it is. The word *vessel* may be a bit antiquated, but it's sufficient to describe a container for water or a beverage. When it's taken in the context of the art, it has a deeper metaphorical meaning—the artist is the vessel that holds the creative spirit.

There's a big difference between taking a sip of water from a cheap plastic cup and drinking from a glass goblet in your favorite color with diamond-shaped facets that catch the light. There are aesthetic differences, but there's much more. Drinking from a glass you don't like could distract you from the creative flow. Your thoughts could spiral into thinking about a barista or going to another coffeehouse. You might see a design or a color you don't like on a can that shuts down the flow. A cheap plastic cup may feel weak in your hands, and you might think about how it's affecting the environment just as the creative spirit was about to tap on your shoulder. On the other hand, drinking from a glass that doesn't distract you will keep your energy focused and lifted.

You have many options to consider. You can choose something you love, in which case, it'll inspire you every time you drink. You could choose something that aligns with your project, such as a souvenir from a production you're recreating. Another choice is a container with magickal symbols or words on it, which enhance the energy of your beverage. The last choice is to go neutral, such as a clear glass. This isn't really a creative correspondence, and it's only recommended when distraction is a major problem and other options don't work. Evaluate the container's color, size, material, texture, shape, and design. Once you find something that works, stick with it. The most important aspect of your container is that it supports you to continue creating.

CREATIVE RITUAL:
SPIRIT, AIR, FIRE, AND WATER

Go to your art workplace and minimize distractions. Organize and tidy up, and then clear your mind. Welcome the creative mindset within and the creative spirit.

Light the incense or use the essential oil. Let the aroma inspire you. Play inspiring music or other sounds and allow your energy to shift to get into the mood of your project. Review your brainstorm sheet and any notes you've taken recently.

Hold your lighter or matches and feel the creative potential within you. When you are ready to activate it, light it up. Enjoy the light of the flame, then light your candle. Feel your inner passion glow.

Make a beverage in a mug or cup that inspires you. Hold the cup and think of the creative spirit's association with water. Ask the beverage to bring the creative flow to you. As you drink it, briefly go over your outline and feel a sparkle of confidence in your ideas. Get in touch with what you love about your vision. Write down any other ideas that come to you on the outline.

• *Shower Spell* •
INSPIRATION AND DISSOLVING BLOCKS

Water cleanses and restores our emotional balance, and it can also inspire us when we're feeling blocked. The most prolific artists I know have a daily cleansing routine that includes a shower. When we cleanse ourselves, it does more than just wash the external layer. A deeper cleansing occurs too, in which our overthinking, negative emotions, and creative blocks all start to dissolve. Cleansing is important in magick, so it makes sense to cleanse ourselves for creativity as well. This practice gives your mind a break, which can open the floodgates of inspiration. Although this is a shower spell, you can use it in a bath too, if you wish. All you need for this spell are water and soap with an aroma that inspires you, such as lavender or orange. For scent suggestions, see chapter 2 and the "Aromas for Creativity" section. You may want to have a notebook nearby in case inspiration strikes while you're in the shower.

Step into the shower or bath. Allow the warm water to flow over you. Inhale deeply and feel your creative block. Call to your body any emotions you feel about it, such as frustration, stress, worry, confusion, or doubt. Talk about your creative block and name your feelings out loud. Exhale deeply and let go of your concern for the moment. Use the soap to begin to wash up and imagine that whatever is holding you back is slowly washing off you. If you're in the shower, imagine your creative block and feelings going down the drain, far away from you. Rinse off and imagine whatever is blocking you is gone from your body, either down the drain or in the bathwater. Place your hand over the drain (or if you're in the bath, put your hand over the tub of water). Push out any remaining energy you wish to purge from yourself through your hands and down the drain. Say, "Creative block, you're gone from me, never to be seen again! For I am cleansed and feeling free, and you are going down the drain."

Let your mind drift into a daydream state as you continue to wash up. This is when the magick happens, so don't skip this step. When you're done, step out, towel off, and walk away. If you don't get insights about your block at this time, try to find the daydream state the next time you shower or bathe.

Tips for Flowing Creativity

- You may recall from the introduction that art is like a spell cast by the artist, and anyone who partakes of it falls under its influence. Take a moment to figure out how you want your audience to feel. Imagine a beginning for your art that will cast the right spell to evoke that emotion within whoever interacts with it. If you wish, you can do an extra brainstorm with the opening and the emotion or theme to get ideas about it.

- For an elemental boost, use water charged with moonlight or sunlight to cleanse your creative workplace and recharge items. You can use them in your art too, such as when you rinse paintbrushes or sponge water onto clay.

- Write down your dreams upon waking for insights about creative blocks. If you encounter a blocked feeling in your dreams and you didn't work through it, work through it in your life or your art.

- Find your way into your art by playing with it. Starting a session badly is better than not starting at all. Sometimes what we think is bad turns into a great session. I once lived across the street from a brilliant pianist who started every session with random poundings on the keys. After several minutes of playing, those terrible noises found a rhythm and turned into the most beautiful songs.

- Create art you love. You'll get much more enjoyment out of it, and you can depend on that feeling.

Let Go with the Flow

Emotions are an important part of creativity, but you don't need to feel totally healed before you can create. That's an impossible state, so know that you are worthy to create as you are. Continue to seek the flow and remain open to the creative spirit. With repeated encounters, you'll get there, and your creative project will give you a feeling of deep emotional satisfaction.

CHAPTER 5

Earth: Growth and Perseverance

It's time to bring the dreamy vision of our art down to earth and into a more grounded expression. With every session, brush-stroke, or word, we make our art more real. Earth is the perfect element to help us do this work. It helps us find sustained energy as we lay down the bones of the rough draft. This is no small feat, and in many ways, it's utterly magickal.

This chapter and the next encourage you to create an early version of your complete art. For simplicity's sake, this book calls it a rough draft, but you can call it anything that fits your art. A performer might call it a first run-through, musicians could call it a beta recording of the album, graphic artists would try their hand at the rough sketches, makeup artists might call it a trial look, and designers could make a test sewing of their clothing line. Whatever you call your first version, you'll create it as best you can with a little encouragement and assistance. Your art will probably be far from done, but you'll be able to see, hear, or feel what works and what doesn't. That's knowledge you can use as a solid foundation to build up more of what does work on the journey to make your art complete.

If possible, refrain from changing or revising too much at this stage, especially if you're a beginner artist. If you're anything like me, you might want to test this theory. I can tell you from experience that it's far better to have a rough idea of the big picture of your art and revise it later rather than making changes when you don't have the full overview. What good is a perfect opening scene when you don't know what happens in the finale? There's a good chance that your opening scene will change drastically by the time you finish, so your perfect opener will be useless. This has happened to me more often than I like. Trust me—it's a good idea to finish your rough draft. Even if your goal is to only make one ceramic wall hanging, you should finish sculpting it, coat it in glaze or slip, and fire it in a kiln to see what the end product really looks like as opposed to what's in your mind. Finishing a project is one of the biggest hurdles for new artists, so it's particularly important to make this step a reality.

Constant revising is one reason why so many beginners' works of art remain unfinished. This is a hard lesson for perfectionists to learn, but it pays off, especially when you actually have a finished product that you created on purpose and not by chance. There will be plenty of time to revise your rough draft after it's complete (this will be covered in chapter 8, "Creative Alchemy"). For now, let's delve into all the ways that the element of earth can inspire us to get to work on making our dreams a reality.

The Creative Journey

Some creators get overwhelmed when they think about all the tasks they must do for their project. This kind of a list can seem insurmountable, but it's not. The fact that someone else has done it means you can do it too. The big secret to being an artist is that it's all about the journey. That's where the magick is—in the day-to-day accumulation of skills and progress.

Being an artist is like being the hero in a magickal world where anything you desire can be brought to life. You'll be presented with tasks that could be perceived as work, or they could be viewed as fun challenges that you get to solve to get to the next level. You make the choices, and you decide where to go.

What's the best way to start a journey? You'll need a map or a vision of where you'd like to go. We accomplished that in chapter 1. You'll need courage and emotional clarity, which you stoked in chapters 2 and 3. Now, you have to show up and take one step toward your goal. And then another. And then another.

As you continue along the journey, you may need to pause for a moment to learn more information about the journey ahead and maybe change your course to one that's more attractive to you. Take the time you need to correct your map, and then get back on the path. The deeper you go into this world, the more magick it will reveal to you. Further along on the path, your creative spirit awaits, ready to give you inspiration and energy. However, it only shows up when you do. Are you ready to show up?

THE MAGICK OF ENDURANCE

As artists create their art, they learn a lot about themselves and the nature of their art. They understand their interests and how they want to express their art through style, and they also learn about their limitations. There's a theory that the greatest artists become good only after they create for over 10,000 hours.[57] This huge chunk of time seems to rewire their brains to form connections between the executive parts of the brain and the imaginative parts. It may seem like a lot of time, especially if you're a

---

57. Gladwell, *Outliers*, 39–55.

beginner, but don't let it intimidate you. Many people become wonderful artists in far less time, especially if they've had other artistic ventures previously. Even if you haven't, don't be discouraged. We all start somewhere. Even the mighty oak tree started as an acorn. No one asks the acorn why it's not an oak. Have patience, show up, and you will persevere.

• Spell •
Acorns for Patience and Growth

This spell allows you to see your growth and envision the steps it takes to get there. It's especially magickal for people who need grounding and patience. It can also help you build more trust with the natural process of life. Acorns are used in this spell because oak trees correspond with magick and wisdom.

Materials
a couple of acorns with no holes or cracks
glass of water
potting soil
medium-size pot about 8 inches in diameter
drip saucer

Remove the caps from the acorns and place the nuts on your desk. Drop the acorn nuts into the glass of water and leave them there for twenty-four hours. Discard any floating acorns, as they won't grow. Prepare the pot by placing the potting soil in the pot and leaving an inch between the lip of the pot and the soil. Hold an acorn in your hands and say, "The power of the mighty oak lies within this seed. Teach me trust and patience as you grow into a tree."

Poke a hole in the soil about an inch and a half deep and plant the seed. Place the drip saucer beneath it. Water your acorn with the water in the glass (which represents the creative flow), and then continue to water about twice per week or whenever the soil is very dry. Place the pot in sunlight. For the next few weeks, trust that the acorn is doing what it needs to do to become established in the soil, even if it doesn't appear to be making any progress right now. Within a few weeks, you'll see a tiny shoot of growth. Continue to have patience and trust as you water your tree of wisdom.

The Magick of Physically Showing Up

There's a concept in the writing community called "ass in chair." It means the magick can't happen until you're showing up and in position. It's an effective idea because it evokes the physical aspect of how most writers write. It basically says that you can have inspiration, passion, and the creative flow, but if you're not sitting in your writing chair, you won't move the needle of progress. When writers sit in their chairs, they create a physical cue for their bodies to know it's time for the creative work to begin. It also gives a signal to the creative spirit that they're ready to engage with them. When artists show up in their creative position, they can conjure their abstract vision of their project, receive energy from the creative spirit, and translate it to make a finished product. This is nothing less than pure magick.

If your art doesn't happen when you're sitting in a chair, come up with a different phrase. For example, a painter could say "brush in hand." A dancer might prefer "standing in position one." After you do all the other actions in the creative ritual, show up physically with your phrase and allow the creative work to begin.

HONOR YOUR BODY

It's so important to take care of your body while you create. Sacrificing your health for your art is a detrimental concept. A balanced, healthy life will always sustain you and your art in the long run. One of the best ways to keep your energy flowing is to warm up with light stretching or exercise before your session. Wear clothes that are comfortable and help you show up. This could mean wearing the same outfit to reduce the number of decisions you have to make. Every hour or so, take a short break to refresh yourself. Walk around, stretch, and hydrate. Get a snack if you're hungry, and then go back to continue creating, if possible. When you feel tired or you can't focus as much, it's time to stop.

It's important to get a variety of physical experiences. Breakthroughs often happen when we give our bodies rest and the physical opposite of our arts. For example, if you write in a sedentary position, be sure to move your body. You could take up walking, dance, martial arts, or riding a bike. If you use your hands a lot in your art, make sure you let your hands have a break. If you're physically active in your art, such as in dance or figure skating, do something where you can be still, such as reading, bathing, or getting a massage. This opposite experience can inspire us to no end.

As you work, be aware of what times you connect with the flow. You'll know it's a good time for you because it'll feel easier and more productive. Try working during those times regularly and see if you can repeat the experience. If so, think of this time as one of your other creative correspondences. It's tempting to think that the best time to create is when the creative spirit knocks on your door with a bouquet of ideas. Sometimes, this will happen, but don't wait for them to come to you. Do the creative ritual, get in position, and dive into your work.

A LITTLE REST

After a creative session, it's important to rest. This can shift your brain and body from the intense creation mode into something easier to sustain. It lets you wind down and feel normal after a big session. The earth knows all about the cycles of productivity and rest. There are daily cycles, such as day and night, and there are the longer cycles of the seasons too. Good artists know to follow the same patterns when they appear in our bodies. Our bodies and minds might have their own cycles of productivity and rest. These may differ from day to day and week to week. There may be a time when you simply can't create. A sickness, an immune system flare-up, grieving, or having a natural low time are all signs for us to rest and not push ourselves.

Generally, you'll know you need restorative rest when you find yourself groaning or clenching your muscles in protest whenever you think about doing anything. This is your body's way of asking for a break. Pushing yourself at these times won't yield the best results. The best thing you can do is to take it easy and take care of yourself. If you find yourself spacing out, this could be a sign that you need a mental break. I say let yourself space out for a little while. All too often, we stop ourselves from daydreaming when we probably need it. If creativity is closer to an animistic state of mind, we may need to just let ourselves be for a while. When this happens, instead of pressuring yourself to tune into your project, spin the metaphorical dial and tune out. Find a different station, perhaps one with only static. Give your brain the space it needs. You'll likely come back to your project with more inspiration than before.

REST AND REWARD

One of the most effective ways to feel refreshed after creative work is to combine rest with a reward. There's nothing like looking forward to eating chocolate and reading a good book, taking a walk with a friend to a coffeehouse, taking a luxurious bath, or watching television with a small bowl of ice cream. This combination of resting while enjoying a reward incentivizes you to do the creative work. Your reward should be satisfying on multiple levels, so use whatever gives you the sense of reward and keeps you creating. It should go without saying that rest is not a reward. It's a regular part of life. Resting after creating should never take the place of regular rest, which you can take anytime without "earning" it.

When I was first creating, I gave myself visual rewards to track my progress and keep going. Every time I worked on my project for an hour, I drew a star on my calendar. It was an instant reward with virtually no cost whatsoever, and it felt so satisfying to see my progress. If you lose track of time easily, this is the perfect way to make sure you're keeping up with your schedule. It lets you see your winning streaks and how long it has been since you last worked on your project. Use whatever symbol that means something special to you. Feeling fancy? Use stickers, a marker, or a special pen. These are inexpensive and effective ways to reward yourself.

You can also give yourself a bigger reward for your larger accomplishments. These can be very motivating. Think of something you can give yourself when you finish your rough draft. It should be something you wouldn't normally treat yourself to. That way, it'll be more special and appealing. Try to make it something you can experience and not just consumer goods. You could get a big stack of books from your favorite bookstore, attend an interesting class or a gathering, go on a trip, or buy a luxury item such as a professional massage. Just thinking about your big reward can trigger dopamine, which can motivate you to finish your project.

Tools for Creativity

Your creative tools are the physical parts of your genre. They may be pens, paintbrushes, knives, notebooks, your laptop, or instruments. There's only one rule when it comes to creative tools—they must work. Your tools should be effective. Don't write a novel with a pen that's running out of ink or use a computer from the 1990s that crashes every thirty minutes. These simply don't work well, and in some ways, they're a reflection of your investment in your creative project, or lack thereof. You should like your tools and, ideally, love them. When you love your tools, they'll love you back with greater flow and productivity. Even small upgrades can make a huge difference.

You'll be working magick with these tools, so it's a good idea to cleanse them, just as you would with magickal tools. Cleanse a tool when it's new, whenever someone else has touched it or used it, and whenever its energy feels off or not as conducive. Depending on the art tool, certain methods will be more appropriate than others. For a light cleansing that's generally good for most arts, let wind blow over it, brush its aura with your hands, or blow a few light breaths on it. For a more in-depth cleansing, you can use burning herbs or incense. If your tool is water-safe, you could cleanse it with water charged by the sunlight or moonlight. If you need a refresher on the different types of incense and their properties or how to make charged water, see chapter 1.

For a light cleansing, dip a soft cloth into the charged water, wring the excess water out, and wipe the surface of the tool. Of course, that wouldn't be appropriate for electronic devices like a laptop or an electric guitar, but it could cleanse the dust and energy from a paintbrush or a clay knife.

You can bless your tools with a specific energy by setting them out in the sunlight for a short time, though this generally isn't recommended for electronic devices due to overheating. Moonlight is a safer option. If your tools are small enough to fit on a windowsill, set them up to soak up the energy overnight when the moon is full or nearly full. Consider placing crystals and herbs with them to boost the energy even more. If your tools don't fit on a windowsill, place them on a table or a desk near an open window where moonlight shines in.

The so-called "writing life" is basically sitting on your ass. ... My muse may visit. She may not. The trick is to be there waiting if she does.
—STEPHEN KING

The spirits of a place can bless your art tools with magick if you gain their favor. They're pretty powerful at granting wishes, so it's worth it to try. Bring an offering for the spirits as well as your tools to a location that inspires you. Some ideas could include a playhouse, a museum, a musical venue stage, a forest, or a library. Find a place to stand or sit for a while. Relax your body and feel the energy of the place. Try to sense echoes of what has happened there recently—has it been a busy place or a rarely visited one? Has a performance or a special exhibit recently taken place? When you feel you understand the energy, imagine what the spirits there would like as an offering, and if it's possible, give it to them. This could mean picking up trash, sending heartfelt admiration and awe to the spirits, gifting water or crushed herbs to a forest tree, organizing a bulletin board, or playing music and doing a little dance. Anything that you can do to raise the energy of the place could feasibly work as an offering, as long as you feel comfortable doing it and it's legal. After your offering, place your tools somewhere prominent so they can soak up the energy. For example, you could set your flute case on the stage for a moment, set your laptop against a giant tree that emanates ancient wisdom, or secretly place your clean paintbrush against the outside wall of a museum. Tell the spirits of the place what you want to do with your art and ask them to bless your art tools.

Awaken the spirit of your tools by talking with them and asking them for assistance with your projects. When you see them or begin a session, welcome them with a smile, just as you would an old friend. At the end of a session, thank them for the assistance and say goodbye to them.

Rituals are another way you can bless your art tools with more energy. You can try using your stylus pen as a wand or an athame. It may or may not work, but you won't know until you try. Alternately, you could have a ritual to bless your tools. If you try this, direct the energy you raise into your tools instead of out into the world. Your tools can absorb the energy, and depending on the strength of the ritual, they can carry it for a long time before needing to be charged again.

Caring for your creative tools is similar to caring for magickal tools. Don't use your creative tools for any other purposes unless you're okay with them being associated with that energy. As a writer, I'm especially careful with the pens I use for brainstorming and writing notes. Whenever I pick one up, part of me knows it's time for creative work. There's a lot of intention built into it. You'll also want to be mindful of how your tools are stored after use. I cleanse mine often, and when they're not in use, I store them or cover them with a cloth so they're hidden from view. I'm also careful who I loan them to because the borrower may change the energy of the tool in some way. These habits may seem excessive, but when I was careless about them in the past, I was thrown off my creative vibe. It's better to be safe than sorry.

Creative Correspondences for Earth: Crystals and Herbs

All kinds of artists use magickal items around their workplaces to inspire their creativity. The painter Remedios Varo placed several crystals and stones beside her whenever she painted.[58] Likewise, Mickie Muller uses herbs that correspond to her project when she paints. I use both crystals and herbs, which are set up on the corner of my writing desk. My favorites are amethyst, hematite, and sodalite. I also have mint, bay laurel, and rosemary in a bowl nearby. As you read these herbs and crystals, take note of any that inspire you.

CRYSTALS

Crystals are mineral formations, some of which are millions of years old. These multifaceted wonders are often unearthed from the deepest and darkest places. Some formed under metamorphic conditions of intense pressure and heat. Many people associate crystals with the underworld and ancient forces of nature. As such, they carry timeless wisdom about patience, complexity, and depth. Whenever possible, try to find crystals that were ethically sourced.

All the following crystals correspond with creativity.

---

58. Grossman, *Waking the Witch*, 183.

CRYSTALS FOR CREATIVITY

Agate, Fire: Inspiration, confidence, logic, passion, grounding, confidence

Calcite, Orange: Confidence, insights, enthusiasm, motivation, communication, willpower

Carnelian: Inspiration, enthusiasm, optimism, clarity, empowerment, balance, memory

Citrine: Energizing, releasing old beliefs, power, self-esteem, productivity, purpose

Fluorite: Balancing, concentration, expression, learning, memory, mental abilities

Garnet: Grounding, stamina, passion, energizing, optimism, organization, memory

Hematite: Grounding, drive, calm, focus, memory, discipline

Howlite: Calm, concentration, mental healing, memory, learning skills

Jasper, Red: Deep focus, courage, connection with the world, minimizes distractions

Kyanite: Balance, self-expression, mental clarity, memory

Pyrite: Memory, learning, confidence, grounding

Ruby: Concentration, ability, power, stamina, passion, optimism

Sodalite: Communication, confidence, learning, order, mental abilities, imagination

Topaz (Blue): Removal of mental blocks, authenticity, confidence, memory

Topaz (Golden): Willpower, action, authenticity, expression, communication

HERBS

Herbs are the opposite of crystals, in some ways. They're living, breathing plants that grow on the earth's surface. They experience the elements of wind and rain as well as the daily cycles of the sun and night. The life cycles of most herbs aren't terribly long—many only last until frost. Herbs have the energy of growth, the living earth, tenderness, and balance. Their wisdom is about maintaining the proper conditions for growth, not going to excesses, and keeping up with daily schedules. They encourage us to weed out errant thoughts from the garden of our minds so our projects don't get choked out. Last, they encourage us to roll up our sleeves and dig, but only as deep as their roots go. Anything deeper isn't within their purview.

All the following herbs correspond with creativity.

HERBS FOR CREATIVITY

Adder's-Tongue (*Ophioglossum*): Creativity, words, healing (poisonous if ingested)

Bay Laurel (*Laurus nobilis*): Vision, wisdom, focus, associated with the Muses

Carnation (*Dianthus caryophyllus*): Strength, balance (poisonous if ingested)

Cinnamon (*Cinnamomum verum*): Vision, inspiration, power (if used internally, use in moderation)

Damiana (*Turnera diffusa*): Creative flow, spirit communication

Eucalyptus (*Eucalyptus*): Clarity, focus (poisonous if ingested)

Feverfew (*Tanacetum parthenium*): Inspiration

Passionflower (*Passiflora*): Inspiration, calming (leaves are poisonous if ingested)

Rosemary (*Salvia rosmarinus*): Memory, concentration

Saffron (*Crocus sativus*): Passion, mental healing

Spikenard (*Aralia racemosa*): Protection, spirit communication, strength (may be poisonous if ingested)

Witch Hazel (*Hamamelis*): Passion, clearing negativity, confidence, power (if used internally, use in moderation)

Creative Ritual: Spirit, Air, Fire, Water, and Earth

Go to your art workplace and minimize distractions. Organize and tidy up, and then clear your mind. Welcome the creative mindset within and the creative spirit.

Light the incense or use the essential oil. Let the aroma inspire you. Play inspiring music or other sounds and allow your energy to shift to get into the mood of your project. Review your brainstorm sheet and any notes you've taken recently.

Hold your lighter or matches and feel the creative potential within you. When you are ready to activate it, light it up. Enjoy the light of the flame, then light your candle. Feel your inner passion glow.

Make a cup of tea or some other beverage. As you drink it, go over your outline and feel confident in your ideas. Feel the alluring draw of your art. Get in touch with what you love about your vision. Write down any additional ideas that came to you on the outline.

Place your crystals and/or herbs nearby and use them to help you find the right energy in your body for doing the work. Use your special phrase—ass in chair, brush in hand, etc.—and start to work. Stay open to the influence of the creative spirit. Take short breaks and get back to your project until you feel it's time to stop. Track your progress and treat yourself to a little reward.

• *Exercise* •
THE MAGICK OF SCHEDULING

The most prolific creators set goals, make a detailed schedule, and stick to them. Your goals should be a bit of a challenge, but still implementable.

State your big goal, such as writing a 50,000-word book or composing an album with twelve songs.

_____

_____

_____

_____

When do you want to complete the rough draft of your art?

_____

_____

_____

_____

How many days per week will you devote to it?

_____

_____

How many hours per session will you work on your art?

_____

_____

_____

_____

What problems do you foresee that could arise with this schedule?

_____

_____

_____

_____

How will you deal with these problems so you stay consistent with your goals?

_____

_____

_____

_____

Envision yourself showing up and accomplishing every task that's necessary for you to create. Envision the results. Ground that feeling into your body and allow it to drive the project forward. Write down what this looks like for you.

_____

_____

_____

_____

Tips for Grounded Creativity

- There are all kinds of practices to bring about good creative work. Before you accept anyone's creative advice as the only way to create, feel whether it rings true for you. Don't feed bad if it doesn't yield fruit. You're not a failure if someone else's method isn't advantageous. There's a whole spectrum of artists in the world, and what's useful for one will not necessarily be useful for another. The best creative practices are those that set you on the path to find the creative spirit.

- Back up your work in multiple places. Make copies and take photos whenever possible. Use a cloud-based server such as Dropbox in case you lose the physical parts of your project. Save your backups often with the current date in the file name.

- Some artists prefer to end their work session on a final note, such as completing a chapter or a portion of their art. They do this so the next time they work, they can start with something new. Other artists purposefully leave their work half done because it's easier for them to pick up where they left off or see what needs to happen next. Try both methods and see what works.

Grow On

Be patient with yourself during this phase. You're giving life to a dream. Endurance comes from regular effort. Even if your session only moves your journey forward a tiny bit, those little changes eventually add up to produce big, noticeable effects. Remember to look back at how far you've come, then take another step.

CHAPTER 6

Casting the Circle: Finishing Your Rough Draft

There's an ancient symbol common in alchemy: the ouroboros, or the snake eating its own tail. I interpret the ouroboros to mean that there's a multidimensional kind of wholeness that is experienced through the completion of cycles. This is a beautiful and moving sentiment, and it often inspires me to finish my rough draft. However, when I'm struggling, I can't help but think about the snake before it became the ouroboros. Maybe it chased its tail in a circle for a while without chomping into it. Perhaps it took an unexpected break to shed its skin. There may have been days when it stretched so it could work on its circle. Maybe it tried again, failed, and gave up for a while, only to try again because the thought of completing it was too alluring. This time, when the snake tried again, something was different. It was easier to form the shape. The concentric slithering came more naturally, as if it had known how to do it all along. When the snake finally reached its tail while in the shape of a circle, it bit down with a sense of triumph and accomplishment. Only then did it become the ouroboros.

Closing the loop on a project can often feel intimidating because, like the snake, we're chasing after our own elusive endings. We may not know how it'll work, and we could doubt that our art will ever be complete. If you're feeling this way, relax. It's all part of the process. If my decades of creative experience have taught me anything, it's to keep going. When the end is so close, we can rely upon our training to make the final lunge and, eventually, reach the end.

The Magick of Ending

Completing your rough draft is sort of like casting a circle. You started at the beginning, made your way through the elements, and added the final touches to make it magickal. Some artists find that their endings recall the beginning scene or feeling, but with a different twist. Finishing your project is like returning home after all your adventures. You're not the same person you were before you ventured out, and it shows. There are some changes about you that may not be noticeable at first. I believe anyone who experiences the creative spirit carries a bit of the otherworld with them.

Consider the circular concept in your art. If you're painting a series, the last painting can recall the first, but with an expounded theme. If you're a dancer, the last pose could echo the first but with some significant change. It's all about showing some meaningful change in your art.

• Exercise •
BRAINSTORMING THE COMPLETED CIRCLE

In creativity, the circle represents wholeness as well as the beginning, the middle, and the end of your art. This exercise builds on the brainstorming concepts you came up with in chapter 2. It'll take them to completion, with a greater sense of well-roundedness.

You'll use the concept of a completed circle in your art to promote a sense of progress, balance, and completion. Ideally, it'll clarify the emotional journey your audience will take with your art so they feel more satisfied and elevated.

The completed circle represents different journeys to different artists. Some examples are a collection of paintings or sculptures, a fictional journey, a dancer's depiction of a story, an album, the chronology of a fashion show, and so forth. This exercise should also give you ideas about how to end your project, whether it's a large project or a small one. Even if you only make one small work of art, such as a poem or a small sculpture, these concepts can be useful. However, it may not be helpful for all artists, and all aspects of it may not be usable by all artists. Anyone who has limited input or freedom on their art may not benefit from it because their art has already been defined for them. Likewise, anyone who has monochromatic art may not be able to use the contrasting point, and the ending concepts may not be useful for artists who make three-dimensional works because their beginning is the exact same thing as their ending. Nonetheless, this exercise is included in the hope that it'll be useful to the artists who can use these concepts.

Materials
sheet of paper
pencil with an eraser
colorful marker

Draw a medium-size circle with a pencil and make a small X at the top of it. This X represents the first impression from the audience. It should be something captivating that makes the audience want more. This can translate to the first painting in the gallery, the most striking feature of a three-dimensional work of art, the opening scene of a play or dance, the first paragraph of a novel, and so forth. To the right of the X, write down some details about what will be revealed upon first impression—the image, scene, feelings, colors, characters, words, and anything you can think of.

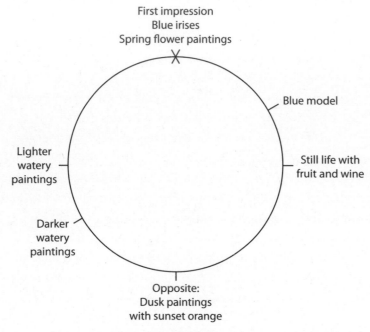

First impression
Blue irises
Spring flower paintings

Blue model

Lighter watery paintings

Still life with fruit and wine

Darker watery paintings

Opposite:
Dusk paintings
with sunset orange

Figure 2: Circle Brainstorm

On the other side of the circle from the X, make a small line. This is the contrast point, or the divergence from expectations. It's useful for artists to show something within the same world, but with a different spin. It's often a surprise that adds intrigue and mystery to the work. Beside the line, write the opposite of what you wrote for the beginning—the opposite feeling, scenery, colors, images, situations, characters, or whatever comes to mind.

For three-dimensional artists, this could be the opposite side of their sculpture—if the front of a creature is the introduction, the tail and back would be the opposite. For musicians, it could be a different take from the introduction. Write a few more notes about what it means in the context of your art. If you're unsure, simply write down whatever ideas come to you. You can always erase the ones you don't use.

Make a line on the circle just to the left of the X. This is your ending or your finale, where you'll bring the concept of your art back to the first impression, but with a difference that shows the journey of the art. To the left of this mark, write variations of the beginning themes with additional details about the ending.

Add more lines around the middle of the circle. Beside them, write in details about the progression of your art from the introduction to the contrast point in the middle (going clockwise), and from the contrast point to the end. Keep writing notes around the circle to develop the middle parts of your idea.

Let this sheet of paper sit for a couple of days so you can gain a bit of objectivity. You'll probably come up with some great ideas in the coming days. Feel free to add them, but don't get too deep into it. After two or three days, review this sheet. Erase the ideas you don't like, and with a colorful marker, circle the ideas you like the most. This is your road map for completing your project. Place it somewhere you'll see it often so you'll be reminded of it.

Creative Circle Groups

Over the ages, artists have used groups to help them complete their work. When other artists show up, inspiration flows freely, there's accountability about your progress, and you share in a camaraderie of the medium. A creative circle is a group of supportive artists who help you show up to your project and make headway. Your conversations can teach you a lot about the creative process and how we all experience it. These people will share in your celebrations during joyous times, and they'll commiserate during defeats. You can share resources and talk each other through creative blocks. The best part about them is that you don't have to believe the same things or even work on the same kinds of projects. Your circle only needs to show up to make the magick happen.

MEETUP SESSIONS

In a live group, you and other artists meet somewhere and work on your projects at the same time. The main goal is to show up, share space, and encourage creativity. These meetings usually happen in person, but they can also be streamed on a live video session with or without cameras on. I recommend having a routine of catching up on how everyone has been fairly quickly, and then each person should give a summary of what they're working on that lasts no longer than a minute or two. After that, everyone begins their work, and there's no additional talking unless it's necessary. The group can work in silence, with their own music, or music the entire group can listen to, as long as it's inspirational for everyone. The meetings should be scheduled on a regular basis for the best results.

Some artists like the idea of setting a timer for thirty minutes or an hour or so. When the time is up, the group reconnects and shares how it went. The creators can discuss if they want a break to refresh themselves, or the timer can be set again, and another work session can begin. However, other artists work better without a timer, especially if they go deep into a trance to find their flow. For this kind of group, a set start time and ending time are ideal. Everyone should take breaks as needed without checking in with the other artists and sign off with a message if the other artists are still creating.

REST SQUAD

The rest squad group is similar to the meetup group, but there's an end goal: to rest and recuperate together afterward. These artists convene in person in the same area, such as a house, an artist's studio, or a school. They catch up and discuss their projects for a short while, then break to work on their art in separate areas with no communication. This lets them create for long periods with no distractions. Whenever they feel tired and can't create anymore, they go to a common area such as a living room, a restaurant, or a coffeehouse. They can eat, drink, and partake of entertainment such as a television show or a video. The goal is to have a communal experience to relax the mind and the body. Ideally, the other artists will arrive around the same time, but it doesn't always happen that way. Even if no one shows up to the rest squad at the same time, the rest should still be refreshing enough to continue to create for another session. This kind of community is most helpful for artists who are easily distracted, those who have big projects, or for those who need their own spaces.

CHECK-IN CIRCLE

A more laid-back kind of creative coven is one in which everyone checks in with each other regularly. They can be held online in a chat group, over email, in a text group, in a social media group, or any other way. The National Novel Writing Month (NaNoWriMo) organization is a good example of a check-in group. They provide a forum for people to connect as well as encouragement and tracking as the writers race to write 50,000 words in one month. If you want to host a group of people with variable goals, you can use a check-in group. Every one to two weeks seems to be a good amount of time because it allows time for creation, shifting schedules, and creative dynamics. On the given check-in day, each artist types a brief message about their life, their progress from last time, and their goal for the next set amount of time. The check-in group is especially helpful for artists who have deadlines or quotas. It gives them accountability—whenever you have to tell someone how much you accomplished, you're more likely to do the work. This is especially true if the group includes someone you admire. It works best when everyone has the same level of productivity. Constant creators will thrive in this kind of group, and people who create erratically will likely drop out. Everyone in the group should be supportive of each other. Any jealousy or judgment will give the group a bad dynamic, and it'll fall apart sooner or later. In those cases, it's best to let the group dissolve and start a new one with caring people. Make sure the group is supportive. If people only message about themselves and their goals, it can seem a little lifeless. Be sure to respond to other people's messages and discuss your life outside of your art. Share in their joys and give them a compassionate ear for their defeats.

COLLEAGUE GROUPS

The easiest group of them all is the colleague group. These are less about working or accountability and more about being social and sharing in the collective creative spirit of the times with other similar artists. Colleague groups encourage a meeting of the minds, where ideas are shared and explored. This kind of group was popular in the 1800s and 1900s, as is seen in the literary groups frequented by writers J. R. R. Tolkien and C. S. Lewis, as well as the French café culture, where painters gathered. Sometimes creative work was shared in these groups to inspire discussion, usually in its final form.

TROUBLESHOOTING CREATIVE CIRCLE ISSUES

As helpful as these groups can be, it's also important to be aware of the potential downsides of creative circles so you're not surprised if or when they appear. Just as in magickal communities, not everyone who joins your creative circle has the best intentions for everyone in the group. You may find that people bring their current project as well as toxic jealousy, animosity, and sabotage. Sometimes, they're aware of their harmful traits to the circle, but often, these motives are hidden from the people who exert them. They may not realize that they're being disruptive or hurtful, especially if they're acting from a wounded place. Keep watch for anyone who doesn't show up continuously, blows off promises to help, rejects others' art, lashes out at or slanders the circle, or attempts to dominate the circle's focus away from making art. You wouldn't accept these actions in a magickal circle, so you shouldn't excuse the behavior in a creative circle. These actions change the energy of the circle from supportive to unsupportive, and anything that's not conducive to the act of creating art literally doesn't work. These issues range from a mild annoyance to deep frustrations that linger in your mind and steal your focus and time. When it's more extreme, it's possible that the offensive person is practicing a form of baneful magic so they can steal energy from artists, whether they're aware of it or not. If the offensive person costs the circle any amount of money, irritation, or emotional harm, they're wasting precious resources that could be directed toward making art. Your art is not worth the drama and the lost time.

If someone is not acting in the best interest of the circle, you may need to take a step back and regroup without the person causing the damage. If you wish, you can have a frank discussion with the member about how you need to focus on your art and not whatever they bring to the table. Give them the option to try again or to socialize with you outside of the creative circle. I've found that most disruptive people often want the second option. This is a great way to keep the sacred energy of your creative circle and retain the friendship with someone who may not be ready for a creative circle. Don't take the actions of a disruptive person personally. It's often more about them and their state than it is about you. Also, keep in mind that the vast majority of groups fall apart or change due to shifting life circumstances. Go with the flow of creative energy and be open to changes so you can sustain your creativity, with or without a circle.

Recognize and Eliminate Distractions from Your Art

There are so many things that could distract you from completing your rough draft. Every month has holidays, planned events, birthdays, work, chores, and other duties. These will always exist, and many of them do need our attention. These are responsibilities, and they can't be eliminated. And then there are distractions—the optional things that come up that have little or nothing to do with your art and get in the way. You can use discernment to know when something actually moves the needle on your project and when it doesn't. This section has a few things to look for and tips on sidestepping them.

RABBIT HOLES

There's a metaphor for researching something that doesn't help you finish your project: going down a rabbit hole. Rabbit holes can be fun to jump into. One bit of intriguing information can lead to another fascinating connection, which can lead to a weird but awesome subject, and before you know it, you're in Wonderland. This may be a beautiful place to find yourself, and it's helpful during the air/imagination phase of the project. However, at this stage, it may not help you complete your project.

It's best to realize when you're going down a rabbit hole. You'll know you're in a rabbit hole because what you're doing or researching has no relevance to your project. By all means, take notes and bookmark websites for anything interesting in case it turns into another project. Then, backtrack to the point where you diverged, and shift back to your project's research. It may be helpful for you to jot down a note of what you need to find and try again.

You may also need to take a break. Sometimes, rabbit holes are attractive because they give us mental space from our projects. Whatever you do, take care of yourself and return to the project at hand. Be aware of side passions and researching too much into them. It can be tempting to diverge from the main goal, and it could help your project, but you need to be aware of how much they waste time if they're not contributing.

MISPLACED CREATIVITY

Are you making cookies instead of being creative? Or are you perfecting your website, creating fashionable outfits, or making videos for social media? Ideas for other creative projects often come up when we're feeling creatively frustrated. They're attractive because they're immediately satisfying. The projects only take a few minutes, and the rewards are nearly instantaneous. Compared to a project that takes months to create, it's easy to see why these are alluring.

It's okay to give in to these sometimes because it's so important to have fun and treat yourself. However, recognize when you're spending a lot of time on those other creative projects. You may need to have an honest talk with yourself about why you're avoiding the art. Is your project too ambitious? Is it too serious and not fun enough? Experiment with changing the vision of your project to find a way through.

Clean Space, Clean Mind

Our homes need so much upkeep, and there's always something in need of cleaning or organization. If the urge to tidy your home or rearrange furniture comes up every time you think about your art project, you're not alone. It's fairly common with creative people who are sensitive to their surroundings, though it isn't an issue for everyone. Considering the chaotic energy that clutter, dirt, and grime have, it makes sense that we'd want to have a clean home and workplace.

The good news is that a little bit of cleaning can actually make you even more creative. Physically changing your environment creates space for change to happen in your life. Tess Whitehurst, the author of several magickal books, including *You Are Magical* and *Magical Housekeeping*, feels the same way: "When you clear the clutter, it becomes exponentially easier to manifest the things you want," which includes a finished art project.[59] I believe cleaning clears up more space in our minds, and this lets us create more effectively as opposed to thinking about a list of tasks.

Writing is the deepest trance state I go into, the most pleasant, and my greatest awareness of outside help and channeling.

—DIANE STEIN

However, it's imperative to not get distracted by cleaning, especially if it's a never-ending list. Constant cleaning doesn't help you finish your art. If you prioritize cleaning everything before you allow yourself to create, you'll inevitably have days where you never reach the end of the tasks, and you won't create. Or you might feel tired by the time you're ready to begin. That isn't the ideal state of mind for creating, and you owe it to the creative spirit and yourself to put your art first at least half of the time.

Unfortunately, if you get swept away by big projects, such as painting your entire house or organizing a big area, you may be avoiding your art. Creative blocks manifest in multiple ways, especially by keeping you busy with endless tasks.

Whenever you get the urge to make big changes to clean up your space, put the goal in perspective with your art goal. Hour for hour, how much time will you allot to each one? Can you do something manageable, say in a couple of hours instead of several weeks? For instance, you could paint one wall instead of painting the whole house. You can hide clutter by tucking items in boxes,

---

59. Tess Whitehurst, "Do the Magic, Then Do the Work," in *Llewellyn's 2021 Witches' Companion: A Guide to Contemporary Living* (Woodbury, MN: Llewellyn Publications, 2020), 225.

and deal with it when you're not creating. You could hire help or ask a friend to help you clean your home so the burden isn't completely on you. It's okay to let some things be a little messy, especially when you're creating. Find a happy medium between making progress on a creative project and having a home that's clean enough in the right places. At the end of your life, would you rather have someone remember how clean your windows were? Or would you prefer to be known as someone whose art changed lives? The latter isn't guaranteed, but it's not even a possibility unless you prioritize your art.

• *Spell* •
Transfer Your Focus

If you find that your focus has shifted to something unrelated to your project, you may need a little extra magick to move the focus from that to your creative work.

Materials
3 dried bay laurel leaves
pen or marker
wide ceramic or metal bowl
tea light candle
lighter
bell with a pleasant sound

On each bay leaf, write, "I focus on my art." Set the bowl somewhere safe, such as a desk or countertop with nothing overhead. Light the tea light candle and set it in the bottom of the bowl. Hold the bay leaves together and raise them so they touch your forehead. Say to yourself three times, "I focus on my art." Take a deep breath, then light the leaves on fire. Hold them over the bowl so it catches the ash. When they're about halfway burned, say,

Cleansing smoke, raise the vibe!
Let creativity come alive!
Unfinished work can be let go
until I have something to show.
I transfer the energy of my other drives
and direct them within so I creatively thrive.

Waft the smoke around the space. If the leaves go out, light them again while saying "I focus on my art" three times. When the leaves have burned out completely, ring the bell throughout the space to clear any remaining energy. Place the bell near your workplace. Any time you need to focus, ring the bell.

Identify and Dissolve Creative Blocks

At this point, creative blocks may appear. They're natural, especially for larger projects. When blocks come up, there is always an answer. You're not stuck. You just slipped off the path. I've dealt with a lot of blocks in my life, and I've learned to roll with them. These are the solutions that worked best for me. Some of them may not seem to be related to art or creativity, but in my opinion, they feed a different part of ourselves that requires nourishment before we can finish our projects.

TROUBLESHOOTING CREATIVE BLOCKS: A CHECKLIST

❑ Have you shown up to your creative workplace showered and in clean clothes?

❑ Have you cleaned and cleansed your creative space?

❑ Are you using the creative ritual?

❑ Have you tried other correspondences for the creative ritual?

❑ Have you tried using headphones for your music?

❑ Have you talked with someone about your creative block, preferably another artist in your genre or medium?

❑ Have you researched the topic of your creative block?

❑ Have you brainstormed or journaled about your creative block?

❑ Have you asked your creative spirit for guidance?

❑ Have you used divination for possible solutions?

❑ Have you taken a break and experienced truly restorative rest?

❑ Have you spent time in nature?

❑ Have you grounded into your body and moved (stretching, dancing, or exercise)?

❑ Are you making art that truly moves you?

❑ Is there another project you'd rather be working on?

❑ Did you set this project down and work on another project?

❑ Have you let your project go cold while you get some space from it?

❑ Is there anything you can change in your project to make it all work? For example, if you're writing a story, changing the ending to something that you'd prefer?

❑ Have you gotten away from your usual places to see new sights and meet new people?

❑ Have you enjoyed any new art lately?

❑ Have you eaten a home-cooked meal?

❑ Have you had a good cry and a hearty laugh?

❑ Have you hugged someone you love recently?

❑ Have you reconnected to the inspiring vision that led you to want to create the project in the first place?

ETERNALLY LEARNING

Some creators spend all their time learning about their art and no time doing it. They believe there's always another book to read or a podcast they need to listen to before they can truly begin. This block is a trap because you may never know everything you need to know. Start anyway. Work even if you feel confused about things. There are some things you can only learn by doing. When you actually do the work, you'll be at a better place for the next time you show up.

PERFECTIONISM

When it comes to your rough draft, having it done is better than having it perfected. It's only a rough draft, so don't pressure yourself to get everything right. There will be plenty of time to revise it after it's done. If perfectionism has you feeling blocked, shift your focus. Instead of trying to do everything the "right way," do what you can, when you can.

BURNOUT

Burnout is a state of chronic exhaustion. It can manifest in the mind, spirit, or body. It feels terrible, like you have no energy to do anything. I recommend avoiding it at all costs. Creating should feel good. It's okay if your journey feels slightly challenging at times, but you shouldn't bring yourself to the point of weariness. Creating should be one part of a diverse and balanced life. I challenge you to do this work while enjoying and experiencing life and while resting when you need it.

Burnout arises when we work too hard or when we've set unrealistic expectations for ourselves. The creative spirit doesn't want that. When we're tired, we misread, we mishear, we're clumsier, and negative emotions are more easily triggered. The creative spirit wants you to be rested so you can hear its messages better. It wants you to experience pleasure so you know how to inject passion into your work. It wants you to do shadow work about why you're pushing yourself to burnout so it can clear the emotions and give you the creative flow. It's okay if you have an obsessive personality—some people can't help that trait. You just have to realize when you're obsessing over something that's bringing you down. Be aware of when you're well-rested too. When you feel expansive and you see your project from a bird's-eye perspective, you may be ready to dive in again.

ANOTHER BRILLIANT IDEA

If you're blocked because another project is giving you all the ideas, take notes and see where it goes. It's hard to force creativity to flow in a specific direction. It may be that another project is more desirable to the creative spirit and you as well. This happened to me when I was trying to write the sequel to my fantasy book. Another idea kept knocking on the door of my mind, and it wouldn't leave me alone. I followed the attraction and wrote. It turned out to be an easier project and far more successful. Sometimes, there's immense value in going with the flow of energy instead of against it. You can always pick up your original project again if you wish.

You could also start exploring a completely different kind of art. If the creative spirit really wants it, listen to it. Sometimes, this will be a fleeting attraction and you'll return to your art. Other times, this will teach you intimate details about something you wanted to learn. You could also meet someone fabulous. The creative spirit has a way of introducing people in odd ways. Indulge them when possible. This is one way to feed the creative spirit the food they love—fresh ideas, full of possibility and intrigue.

A BAD CONNECTION WITH THE CREATIVE SPIRIT

If you're living your best, balanced life and you're still feeling stuck, it could be that you're not communicating well with your creative spirit. Everyone has different ways of communicating, and you and your spirit may not have an established dialogue yet. In times like those, try talking with it. Many other people have in times of crisis. Elizabeth Gilbert credits this with saving her book *Eat, Pray, Love* from a devastating writing block when the spirit prompted her to write it and then didn't show up. She spoke out loud to it and said, "If you want it to be better, then you've got to show up and do your part of the deal, okay?"[60] Ask it what you should do about this, or what if you did that? Ask it about the colors and ideas. After you talk with it, show up at your creative workplace in your position. Listen for its whisper late at night. Avoid alcohol and other drugs that cloud the mind. This can help you be more open to its subtle whispers.

• Exercise •
CROSSROADS TAROT DIVINATION
ABOUT CREATIVE BLOCKS

Sometimes with our art, we arrive at a crossroads, and we don't know which direction to take. During times like these, it's helpful to see the options that are available to you right now. Shuffle your tarot deck while you think about your creative block and all

---

60. Gilbert, "Your Elusive Creative Genius."

the directions you could take. Select one card and place it face down before you. Select four more cards from the deck and place them in the four directions around the first card, face down. Turn the cards over one at a time and read them. The directional cards are the actions you can take.

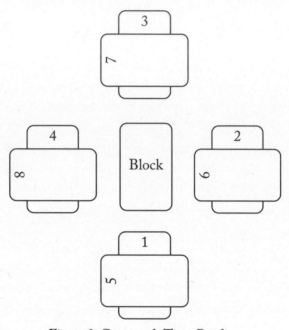

Figure 3: Crossroads Tarot Reading

Block: Who you are and what your block is

Card 1: Path #1

Card 2: Path #2

Card 3: Path #3

Card 4: Path #4

Next, select four more cards and place them over the four direction cards. These crossroads cards represent the other things you should consider on that path. It may be something you have to integrate along with the path or an unforeseen or unintended aspect of taking that route.

Card 5: Crossroads of Path #1

Card 6: Crossroads of Path #2

Card 7: Crossroads of Path #3

Card 8: Crossroads of Path #4

One or two of the paths should stand out as feasible options for your art at this moment. Resolve to take action on that path in the hopes that it dissolves your block. Keep in mind that these paths aren't permanent—new crossroads open up to us all the time. You may also experience walking down one path only to find that it's not ideal. If that's the case, try another path.

Creative Correspondences for the Circle: Holding Space

The circle creates a sacred space, where everything we say and do is amplified. If you don't already, watch what you say about yourself, your abilities, and your project. Be mindful of the energy you bring to your creative workplace. Holding space doesn't have any physical correspondences; rather, it has an energetic one. It's all about believing in yourself. If you feel contracted or stressed about completing your project, hold space for yourself. Allow yourself to expand this energy and unravel the tension. Believe that things will work out. If you can't hold space for yourself, have someone else hold space for you until you get the hang of it.

When you show up for yourself and your work, your magick will come through.

CREATIVE RITUAL:
SPIRIT, AIR, FIRE, WATER, EARTH, AND CIRCLE

Go to your art workplace and minimize distractions. Organize and tidy up, and then clear your mind. Welcome the creative mindset within and the creative spirit.

Light the incense or use the essential oil. Let the aroma inspire you. Play inspiring music or other sounds and allow your energy to shift to get into the mood of your project. Review your brainstorm sheet and any notes you've taken recently.

Hold your lighter or matches and feel the creative potential within you. When you are ready to activate it, light it up. Enjoy the light of the flame, then light your candle. Feel your inner passion glow.

Make a cup of tea or some other beverage. As you drink it, go over your outline and feel confident in your ideas. Feel the alluring draw of your art. Get in touch with what you love about your vision. Write down additional any ideas that came to you on the outline.

Place your crystals and/or herbs nearby and get settled into a comfortable place. Turn off distractions. Set a timer, if you wish. Continue your work and stay open to the influence of the creative spirit. Take short breaks and get back to your project until you feel it's time to stop. Track your progress and treat yourself to a little reward.

Keep showing up with the schedule you made. Hold space for yourself, your art, and the creative spirit. Envision yourself finishing your rough draft and how good that will feel! Allow this satisfying sensation to encourage you to keep it up. If you keep showing up, you'll soon complete the circle with a finished rough draft. It's only a matter of time. Keep going.

• Exercise •
ANTICIPATING COMPLETION

How will you feel when you finish your rough draft? Use descriptive words, such as exhilarated, accomplished, and happy.

_____

_____

_____

_____

What have you finished in the past? For example, a course or degree, another project, and so on.

_____

_____

_____

_____

How did you finish that other project? What kept you going when things got tough?

_____

_____

Can you use the same principles to help you finish this project? If so, how? If not, what can you use?

_____

_____

_____

_____

Tips for Completing the Circle

- Look back to the fire section to see what you wrote about why you want to do this work. These deep reasons can motivate you to finish.
- Do the creative ritual and get to work. You may think that you don't have any ideas or energy, but once you start, you'll probably discover that you can do much more than you believed possible.
- Finish the rough draft. It's a trial run, and it doesn't have to be perfect. It just has to be done.
- Your creative work might feel hard because it's new, but that doesn't mean you're failing. You're developing new routes in your brain to continue the work. Processing takes a lot of energy, so have faith in yourself.
- Don't exhaust yourself to empty. Keep a little creativity juice for next time. It's far easier to recharge a battery with a small charge left rather than one that's completely used up.

Congratulations!

There's nothing like making progress on your project, and completing a rough draft is a huge accomplishment. Now is an excellent time for a short break from creating before you delve into the next step. Rest allows artists to rebuild their stamina and get mental space from their art. Some people even have a term for this: "letting the work breathe." Take a break for a few days or a couple of weeks so you can tackle your project with fresh eyes. If at all possible, don't skip this step. Resting up now means you'll have more mental facilities when you start up again.

Consider dedicating your work to your creative spirit, either publicly or in private. They're the one who helped usher in this vision, so it's fitting to celebrate them at the closing of the circle. In the next section, you'll work on the egregore (the spirit of your art). You'll also use the principles of alchemy to refine it and give it a heart of gold.

PART TWO

Refining and Releasing Your Art into the World

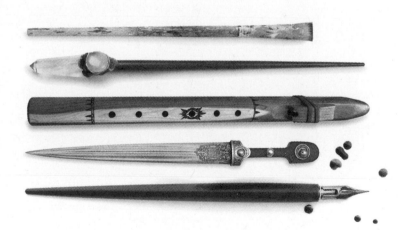

CHAPTER 7

The Spirit of Your Creation: Awakening the Egregore

Whenever we make art, it exists in the material world and the invisible, energetic realm as well. This follows the concept of the Hermetic principle of correspondence: "as above, so below."[61] Think about your favorite painting. It's more than just pigment on canvas, isn't it? It's a whole other world that was created by the artist to capture their ideas and imagination. It may seem like the painting was conjured by magick rather than painted by hand. As the artist created it, they worked with a creative spirit and their vision. They added their thoughts and energy to the painting, and eventually, when it came time to refine the art, they were guided by the art's idea of itself. At a certain point, art takes on a life of its own, which could be interpreted as a spirit. These thought-forms are known as *egregores*, and they're the guiding spirits for the second part of the book. In the terminology of this book, the egregore of your art is not called a creative spirit. They are differentiated because the creative spirit helps you make the art, especially at first, and the egregore is the living spirit of the

---

61. Three Initiates, *The Kybalion: A Study of the Hermetic Philosophy of Ancient Egypt and Greece* (Chicago: The Yogi Publication Society, 1908), 28–29.

art, which only guides artists after the bulk of the work is done and several details are in place.

The Egregore

The word *egregore* comes from the ancient Greek word *égrégoros*, which means "watcher" or "awakened."[62] Egoregres are spirits that exist for everything and every idea, as psychic energies or impressions. They're everywhere—every business, location, person, art, company, and group has them. Egregores can possess a wide variety of energy—from good to bad, helpful to harmful, constant to unsteady, and so on. We interact with egregores several times a day, but most people usually aren't conscious of it.

To illustrate how much we exchange energy with egregores, think of the logo of your favorite coffeehouse. Hold the logo in your mind for a moment. What else did the logo evoke within you? Did you smell the rich aroma of coffee? Did you catch any images in your mind's eye, such as a barista or a display of baked goods? Did you hear any noises? Did you feel a certain way, perhaps more awake or more decadent? If anything at all came to mind in this exercise, you experienced the egregore of that coffeehouse, and maybe the egregore of coffee as well.

These spirits are simple in some ways and complex in others. A personal egregore, known only to one person, can affect them strongly, but its influence on other people may be strong or weak depending on how well other people perceive the egregore. A personal egregore usually exerts a weak influence on the world unless someone has a worldly status. Similarly, when several people hold the same thought about something, those egrego-

---

62. Mark Stavish, *Egregores: The Occult Entities That Watch over Human Destiny* (Rochester, VT: Inner Traditions, 2018), 22.

res can combine to become greater egregores. This happens with worldwide brands, and those spirits influence people daily.

THE EGREGORE OF YOUR ART

You may be wondering how the egregore relates to your art. The answer is simple—your art already has a spirit or an essence. This energy was created the moment you had ideas about your art, and when you finished your rough draft, it was made into a complete but simple spirit.

You might wonder why the egregore is explored in this chapter and not earlier in the creative process. There's a good reason. Artists who become obsessed with the egregore of their project too early often become distracted from finishing it. They try to get all the details about it correct, often overworking a small fraction of their rough draft. That's why it's important to complete the rough draft—because the egregore is a living spirit for your creative work. As chapter 1 of this book touched upon, creative spirits were sometimes thought of as animalistic or mythical creatures. The egregore is associated with animalistic and mythical creatures too. This means that if you only have half of your rough draft, it's like having only half of an animal. It's not alive, and it would be weird to animate the front half of an animal when it doesn't even have hindquarters or a tail. Having a perfect introduction (or head of an egregore) means very little when you don't know what kind of body it has. It's far better to finish the rough draft, from head to tail, even if it's rangy, ramshackle, and it has a bad leg. This way, you can see the shape that your art takes, as well as your egregore, and work from there.

Now that you have a rough draft and a more complete egregore spirit, it's time to refine. As you revise your art, the egregore will begin to help you. It'll indicate what's missing and what needs more work before it's done. This collaborative process is highly beneficial for artists because egregores often inspire them to finish their art. They sustain the artist's vision along with the creative spirit, and they often contribute their own vision of the art as well. This concept of the "art informing the art" isn't new. Michelangelo reportedly said, "I saw the angel in the marble, and I carved until I set him free."[63] In other words, he saw the spirit or living essence within the rough draft. This spirit guided his sculpting with a psychic vision that allowed his eyes to penetrate stone. The vision of the angel or egregore sustained him until he finished the art. When he was done, Michelangelo released the spirit to the world by giving the sculpture to his audience.

Hans Hoffman, an abstract expressionist painter, also believed that artists created living art spirits. He said, "Artistic creation is the metamorphosis of the external physical aspects of a thing into a self-sustaining spiritual reality. Such is the magic act which takes place continuously in the development of a work of art."[64] Egregores continue to help artists create and release their art into the world. As the living, breathing parts of art, they inspire audiences, sometimes moving them emotionally, spiritually, mentally, and physically. The egregore is the key ingredient of your art that makes it completely your own and greater than the sum of its parts. They're also responsible for making art seem magickal and alive—because that's exactly what it is.

---

63. Nils Parker, "The Angel in the Marble: Modern Life Lessons from History's Greatest Sculptor," Medium, July 9, 2013, https://nilsaparker.medium .com/the-angel-in-the-marble-f7aa43f333dc.

64. Hans Hofmann, *Search for the Real*, ed. Sarah T. Weeks and Bartlett H. Hayes Jr. (Cambridge, MA: MIT Press, 1967), 40.

• Exercise •
MEDITATION TO ENVISION
THE EGREGORE OF YOUR ART

For this exercise, you'll need about twenty minutes, a quiet place, your Book of Shadows or a journal, and a pen or a pencil. You may want to record this meditation first so you can go deep into a trance and come back to it whenever you want to commune with this egregore.

Settle into a comfortable position and let go of the day. Start to take long, deep breaths through your mouth. Let your belly fill with air, and then release it slowly and completely. Again, take deep belly breaths that take you into a more serene mindset. Allow your muscles to relax and sink down. Feel your sense of the present moment slip from you until you feel you're between this realm and the next. As you continue to breathe deeply, you find you're in a large room that feels familiar and safe. You feel you've visited here in your dream, perhaps.

Near your feet, you see a fancy, empty box. Somehow, you know you can place your worldly cares in there, just for now. You place your hands over the open box and see your worries and extraneous thoughts flow down your hands and into the box. Close the lid. When you stand up, you feel so much lighter, as if a huge weight has been lifted from you. Walk toward the closed door to the room and stand before it.

Now, think of your art—envision it or hear it. Feel its energy. When you feel its energy within you, place your hands on your head. Imagine your hands are holding a sphere of energy that is your art in your mind, and, gently, move the sphere forward so the energy lands on the other side of the door. Behind that door is the spirit of your art, the egregore of your creation. It's almost ready to show itself to you for the first time.

Knock on the door. If it doesn't reply, wait a moment and knock again, then open the door and look at your egregore as it enters the room. Notice its features and size. Look at its colors. Greet it and ask its name. Listen for its answer. Ask your egregore how it feels about the art. Ask what you can do right now to support it. Respond to it. Ask any other questions you may have.

When you've received your answers, send love and gratitude to your egregore. Tell it you'll visit it again soon. Say your goodbyes for now, then watch the egregore go back through the door. The door closes behind it, and you're left feeling good about your art. Find the fancy box and open it. See your worldly cares there. Take whatever you desire and leave the rest behind. Settle in your original place, and through your nose, take a strong, deep breath. Feel the sensation of your body becoming firmer. Continue your breathing until you feel the sensations of your physical body again, solid and heavy. Feel the clothes on your body and whatever is supporting you. Wiggle your toes and fingers and come back to the present moment.

Write your answers down in your magickal journal or Book of Shadows. It may be helpful for you to draw what your egregore looks like. It's not so important to get it completely right as it is to try. When you revise your rough draft, look over these notes for hints and inspiration. You can repeat this meditation whenever you want to learn more about the egregore of your art.

Feeding the Egregore

The best way to sustain your art's egregore or increase its energy in these early stages is by paying attention to it. Egregores thrive when they're fed energy. They become an even more significant force in your art. It's fairly easy to feed them, and many of us do this activity with several egregores every day. To illustrate how easy this is, we'll return to the egregore of coffee. It's a great example because many of us interact with it on a daily basis. The egregore of coffee is fed by the beliefs you hold about coffee—perhaps that it will make your day better, or that you desire it, or that it's a treat you deserve for doing something you don't want to do. All those thoughts feed the egregore. You also give the egregore energy whenever you buy coffee, which could be seen as a ritual of trading money for the egregore's energy. Making the coffee is another ritual, which involves several steps to achieve the result of partaking in the energy. Last, you feed the egregore of coffee when you take pleasure in drinking it.

There are several ways to feed your egregore. Most of them are easy, and they can be seamlessly adapted into a magickal life (which already has rituals). For me, these practices don't feel draining at all. Rather, they feel like dreamy interludes or a conversation with a good friend. I usually feel more refreshed after an interaction with

> *When and where we create our art magick adds oomph and flavor to the work.*
> —**MOLLY ROBERTS**

them. If you feel the opposite, evaluate if your practice is too strict or if you may have another kind of spirit. Feeding the egregore doesn't need to take a lot of time. Any attention you give it will be effective.

CREATING WITH THE EGREGORE AND THE CREATIVE SPIRIT

The best way to have a relationship with an egregore for your art is to be aware of it whenever you create. You don't have to call upon it, but it doesn't hurt either. When you sit down to your art, take a moment to feel the energy and spirit of your art. Allow the egregore to inform you and direct your actions. At the revision stage of art, the egregore and the creative spirit both arrive to inform the artist about the creation process, but in different ways. The creative spirit feels like an old, wise spirit to me. Conversely, the egregores of my art projects at this stage feel like young spirits. They're easily excited, playful, and energetic. The messages from the egregore feel more physical and emotional rather than mental. It's as if the egregore allows me to feel what the audience will eventually be feeling about the art in the future. Sometimes I catch a glimpse of myself from the egregore's perspective, especially when I'm rehearsing something physical, as in dance and public speaking. There's also a difference in the sensations of the two spirits. The creative spirit feels like a slow but constant trickle that flows down my head and shoulders. Conversely, the egregore feels like a sweeping rush of exciting energy. I feel it more in my heart and my core. While the creative spirit is wonderful at giving suggestions for details, the egregore is more about the big picture or the grand vision. Last, the creative spirit will stay with you throughout different projects, but the egregore is tied to this art project or theme.

One of the biggest challenges when utilizing the egregore is to not let its bursts of excitement distract you. When you expect the egregore to arrive, you won't be shocked by it. Instead, accept the enthusiasm by inhaling it or absorbing it into your energetic field. Let it feed your art with greater intensity rather than throw you off. This may take practice for some people, but many others do it without even being aware of it. Use the egregore's insights to direct your art and the overall vision of your art.

FREQUENT CONVERSATIONS

One way to become more familiar with your art's egregore is to converse with it when you're not creating. It doesn't have to be in a magickal setting. The daily, mundane habit of drinking coffee feeds the egregore of coffee. Think about some everyday activities you can do with your art's spirit to increase its magnitude. As you're doing the activity, simply think of your egregore or your project, particularly as a feeling or how it will be at a future stage. The egregore will give you visions and feelings about it. You can ask it questions or just check in on it. Daydreaming with the egregore is a great practice, especially when it's paired with good music. This semi-meditative practice can easily be adapted into a morning routine or at night just before sleep. You could also think about it when you're on a walk, dancing, or exercising. These interactions don't need to be daily. Any repeated interaction with your egregore will help it grow stronger.

RITUAL

Rituals with the egregore allow artists to maintain relationships with their material and spiritual art. They give us methods for reaching liminal states, where we can have a deeper relationship with the unseen. A ritual with your egregore doesn't need to be complicated. Simple rituals are often the most effective. If possible, adapt the egregore into your regular, personal rituals. You can raise energy with it, have deep conversations with it, and practice divination with it for the project. You could even consciously feed it energy during these times. However, if your rituals are with other people in a closed, intimate setting, it's ethical to ask them if they are okay with you having that energy in their circle. Always consider the other people and their states of mind. Think about the ritual occasion or mood too and whether it's appropriate and conducive for your art or not. For instance, a somber group ritual wouldn't be appropriate or beneficial for the egregore unless it matches the energy of the project.

ALTAR

An altar for your art's egregore is a great way to build energy with it that lasts over long periods of time. Place your drawing of it there as well as any correspondences that remind you of it. For instance, an egregore that has many colors could correspond with a peacock stone. An egregore that looks like a lion corresponds with a stone in that shape or other imagery. You can also add representations of your project, real or fake, such as a homemade ticket for the event or the title of the play written down on a piece of paper. If a physical altar doesn't work for you, create the altar in your mind.

The activities there can vary widely depending on what your goals are. You could hang out with it informally, meditate on how it feels lately, or converse with it. As your creative project develops, you can make offerings for added assistance from it. Unlike the creative spirit, which doesn't need offerings, egregores seem to appreciate them. If your project needs more powers of air, burn incense. Light a candle if you need more passion. Give it a glass of water or another beverage if you need emotional assistance. An offering of food can give you the staying power you need to finish your art. Your offerings don't have to be lavish or extreme. A simple gift of energy, time, or attention is enough to sustain it.

Finishing the Work, Finishing the Egregore

Revising your project under the guidance of the egregore makes it truly come alive. Whenever you notice a change that needs to be made so it fits the greater vision, you're finding the things the egregore needs to thrive after you release it to the world. With every revision to your project, you're creating or improving the parts of the egregore that aren't complete yet. It's almost as if you're constructing parts of their flesh, bones, fur, or scales. Refining another part could equate to enlivening the egregore's eyes with more prismatic colors. Whenever you add extra detail to the work, it shows up in the egregore to make them healthier and more whole. Artists sometimes talk about this part of the creative process with words and phrases like "building the material," "fleshing out the skeleton," and "forming the shape."

With the final revisions, it's almost as if you're listening to the wheezes of life and a faint heartbeat that grows stronger the closer you are to the vision. This phase often makes me think of the saying "The devil is in the details." This appears to have originated as a variant of a German or French proverb that translates to "God is in the detail."[65] Of course, *devil* is another word for a misunderstood god or spirit. However it's defined, it's clear that all those details are necessary to reach the grand vision and inspirit the art.

---

65. Charles Clay Doyle, Wolfgang Meider, and Fred R. Shapiro, *Dictionary of Modern Proverbs* (New Haven, CT: Yale University Press, 2012), 53–54, 103–4.

The Egregore's Evolution

Although the egregore of your art originated in your mind, it'll take on different characteristics when it's released into the world and when other people experience it. A good part of it will still be from you, but it'll be changed by anyone else who thinks about it. You can't take another person's perception of the egregore too personally. We all have preferences about what we like.

The egregore can change over time, and its size waxes and wanes with popularity. If the egregore reaches a lot of people who hold the same thoughts about it, it may become a greater egregore. If people have different opinions about your art, several egregores can develop, and the most dominant one may win out for the majority of people. If the egregore doesn't spread to many people, it'll likely remain closer to your vision.

Sometimes, an egregore takes on a set of characteristics that are the most iconic aspects of an artist or art. For instance, think of Monet's paintings. He produced many works of art, but his *Water Lilies* paintings are the first ones that come to my mind. In this case, the egregore of the *Water Lilies* is so strong that it overpowers the egregores of all his other paintings. This often happens with wide-reaching art.

It's Alive!

Working with the egregore at this stage of your art is like raising a child. You know that it'll eventually be released into the world, but for now, it's your baby. With time and effort, its spirit will grow bigger and stronger. You'll work with the egregore throughout this part of the book. It'll be especially helpful in the next chapter as you refine the rough draft of your art.

CHAPTER 8

Creative Alchemy: Refining Your Art

Alchemy is thought to be a mythical way to turn lead into gold. However, among occultists, it was a metaphor for the spiritual experiments that refined one's magickal abilities and perfected their souls. It's the perfect metaphor for revising our creative work. The artist, like the magician, can use magickal energies like inspiration, imagination, and passion to transform their rough draft. They can work with the creative spirit and the egregore. Finally, they craft a product that is far more meaningful than the sum of its parts. These lessons, in the deeper realms of creativity, are only available to those who have mastered the elemental lessons and completed their rough draft.

The Magick of Revision

No matter what kind of art you create, revision will make it shine. There's magick in bending and shaping our art to suit our visions. It's necessary to shift your internal gears to revise. The part of your mind that held visions and passion to create your rough draft is not the same mindset as the one used for revision. Instead, it uses the more logical or critical parts of the mind. The creative spirit takes a backseat, though it's usually present. It can always chime in with good ideas when it has them. Instead, the egregore guides the artist to make these small changes while thinking about the grand vision.

THE REVISION PROCESSES

Revision usually happens in two stages: rough and fine. The rough stage happens first. It's when you change the big parts of your project that don't work. You may need to add another part or remove an entire section. This process is like replacing broken limbs on the egregore. It means more work for you, but in the end, your egregore will be better off for having had these replacements. The fine revision comes afterward. This is more about refining and polishing the art with little tweaks to make it smoother. Those added details can make the egregore show up with a much greater magnitude.

There are many ways to begin to revise your art. Review the vision statement you wrote in chapter 2. Does your art embody the intentions or the spirit you set out to create? How has it succeeded? Where does it miss the mark? Evaluate what works well and what needs to change.

An outside perspective can help you identify larger problems. How would a random stranger view it? What would they notice first? What would they want to see more of or less? These questions aren't meant to encourage you to make art to please other people but, rather, to get a bird's eye view of it. You can mimic objectivity by putting yourself in the audience or the user's place. Dancers can record a video of their performance where their audience sits and then evaluate whether the dance portrays the vision. Potters can eat or drink from their ceramic ware, and painters can hang their art on a wall to see what it looks like. You can also create this by letting your work go cold. Don't work on it for a couple of weeks and then engage with it. This will allow you to view your work as if you're seeing it for the first time. With all these ideas, look at the big picture objectively to see it from a different perspective. Write down a few ideas about what works and what you'd like to change. These answers will set the tone for your final product.

CREATE REST AND BALANCE

Balance is an important part of natural life. It exists everywhere—in sleep and waking, inhalations and exhalations, night and day, and so forth. Balance is also found in all kinds of art. For example, in visual art, there's a focus area and either a background or the space around it. In fiction, there's a time for action and a time for regrouping. Musicians use silence to enhance the notes even more. In dance, there's activity as well as still moments or small, isolated movements. Balance makes art sing because it's dynamic and it mimics life. Revise your art with this concept in mind.

PERFECTIONISM

When you're revising, the concept of perfectionism will inevitably come up. Scientists know there is no such thing as absolute perfection—it's never attainable. It has no place in magick, art, or nature. Nothing is perfect unless the definition of perfection includes imperfections. Because we're a part of the natural world, it stands to reason that our art shouldn't be expected to be perfect. There may always be room for improvement. Some people spend years revising a single chapter or a dance.

Please resist overworking your art. A few rounds are fine, but too much revision can be like polishing a peach. You'll get limited results after a while, and you may damage the product. Measure how much improvement you're making. When you don't see a big improvement in your results, you're nearly done. Embrace the realization that, eventually, the revision must stop so the art can go to the next stage.

Beta Reviewers

Some artists ask other people for their views on their revised products. These people are known as beta reviewers, and as long as their feedback is helpful, they can help artists. Good beta reviewers are golden. Because they're objective, they can see things the artist missed. They're constructive, they respond in a timely manner, and they're honest. Their comments can make you think more critically about your work. In the end, they improve it. One person's assessment may not be relevant for everyone, but if several people respond to your art with the same comment, pay attention.

There are a few types of bad beta reviewers. The first kind won't like anything about your art, and they won't be shy about saying so. I believe if a reviewer can't critique your art constructively, their advice will probably not be useful whatsoever. This kind of feedback seems to happen most often from strangers who believe themselves to be in the elite class. Do your best to see them for what they are, and don't allow their snide comments get to you. If you don't protect yourself from them, you might feel so angry or defeated that you stop creating altogether. This may be their ultimate motive. Energy vampires and trolls exist everywhere, and they love to destroy hopes and dreams. Whenever you're aware of this happening, refuse to accept their advice. Use magickal protection such as an energetic shield against them, especially if their comments are invasive. Cleansing with burning herbs or a salt bath will also help.

Another kind of bad beta reviewer is the person who loves everything you do, even when it wasn't that great. If they have no comments or suggestions for you at all, don't ask them for advice. What they give you is simply not helpful for the revision process. Don't fault these people for their kindness—instead, use them for support. They'll be good people to lift your spirits if you ever feel down.

The best way to find beta reviewers is to ask for volunteers who partake of your artistic genre and who can give you constructive criticism. There are websites that can provide this kind of review, usually when you trade it with another person. When you have a group, send them a few questions. At a minimum, ask them what's working and what's not working. Include the date you'd like their responses too. Many people will overestimate their ability to respond, so assume only about 60 percent will come through. Reward the betas who come through with a small gift or piece of your art. This will reciprocate the time and energy they gave to you.

THE MAGICK OF REVISIONS: THE TWENTY-FIRST MUG

There's often a big difference between the rough draft and the revised one. This became clear to me when I was dabbling in making pottery on a potter's wheel. The first thing I made was a mug. It was lopsided and the lip was sunken on one side, but it held coffee, and I felt it had a special charm. The next week, I made the same mug again, and this time, it wasn't so lopsided, and the lip was more level. By the time I made the sixth mug, I had changed my method almost imperceptibly, but the mug was much better. I kept at it, making the same kind of mug again and again. Each iteration was slightly different and usually better than the last one. By the twenty-first mug, something had changed. The mug was good. It had the iconic essence of a mug about it. Around the same time, my first mug cracked and broke. It simply wasn't made well enough to sustain the wear and tear.

There's a good chance that your first time trying something won't yield usable results. You might love what you made, but it probably won't stand the test of time. There's a phrase in the creative world—you must kill your darlings. As much as you may love your rough draft, it'll need to change to hold water. Some ideas must be scrapped to make your art stronger. It can hurt to do this, but it's a fairly common concept. See your early iterations as trial runs more than anything else. When you revise and make the next draft, you'll have the experience and skill to make it better.

• Ritual •
BLESS THE EGREGORE
WITH A HEART OF GOLD

As you refine your art more and more, you'll reach a point when you know it's nearly ready to be released into the world. The egregore, the vision, and the project will all merge together into a larger kind of energy that seems to have its own life. You'll know when this happens because your art will move you emotionally. You'll laugh or cry, despite the fact that you created it and you know what happens next. You may have written that chapter, choreographed that dance, and heard that song played hundreds of times before, but when it's done or nearly done, it'll make your heart burn with emotion. Your project will seem to sing aloud, like a bell that has been struck.

This ritual blesses the egregore by giving it more energy and protection. If you wish, you can wait until the next big astrological event, but it's not necessary. Plan for at least an hour. The best place to do it is in your creative workplace. The suggested offerings to the egregore are fruit, nuts, and a beverage such as alcohol or juice, but if your egregore tells you that it likes something else, use it. If possible, go to the grocery with it and ask it what looks good. This is a once-in-a-lifetime event, so it's okay to get something special for it.

This ritual uses a magickal circle for protection against unwanted spirits and to act as a container to raise energy. If you cast a circle another way, feel free to change that part of the ritual. Clear an area so you won't stumble into anything as you work in the circle. You may want to cleanse the workplace before beginning. Gather all your creative correspondences, such as your incense or essential oil, matches or lighter, candle, beverage in a vessel, and crystals or herbs. For this ritual, play music that helps you feel emotional or dramatic—this will assist you with the task of raising energy.

Materials
altar cloth
table
all your creative correspondences
additional candles (optional)
fancy glass
juice or sweet alcohol
fancy dish
fruit and nuts

Make an altar with the cloth and the table. Place your creative correspondences there. Set up the other candles on the altar or somewhere else within sight. Put the beverage and food near the altar, but don't plate it yet.

Face the altar and take in its beauty. If you wish, you can take a drink of the beverage to fully engage with that creative correspondence. Say, "I call upon my guardians, the spirits who protect me, who always work in my favor. Be with me." Draw upon their power and the power of the earth, sun, and moon by breathing in their energy. Fill yourself up with it until you feel elevated.

Face the east and inhale the incense. Feel the inspiration of the creative spirit and the place it usually occupies within you. Say, "I call forth the element of air, with all its inspiration and vision. I ask the spirits of the east to protect this circle."

Face the south and imagine you can feel the flickering of a flame within your heart. "I call forth the element of fire and passion and courage. I ask the spirits of the south to protect this circle."

Face the west and feel the creative flow trickle over you. "I call forth the element of water, with its cleansing, balance, and flow aspects. I ask the spirits of the west to protect this circle."

Face the north. Feel the strength of a mountain within your bones and flesh. "I call forth the element of earth, with its ability to grow and persevere. I ask the spirits of the north to protect this circle."

Face the center and open your arms. "I cast this magickal circle for protection from harm. I cast it to act as a safe and blessed place for my magick. The circle is cast." Envision the circle forming around you. See the sacred space you created here as thick with magick and potential. If you wish, you can pump more energy into it by drawing the energy of the celestial forces into your body through your breath and releasing it into the circle. Take a moment to dance, if you wish.

When you're ready for the next step, say, "I call upon my creative spirit and ask it to join me in this circle. I ask you here for the sacred purpose of creating life within the egregore of my art, the spirit you helped create. I ask you to join me now." Wait a moment until you feel the presence of the creative spirit. "Thank you for joining me."

"I call upon the energy of the egregore of my art. I have envisioned you and worked on my project and worked on completing you at the same time, filling in the gaps between your ribs, completing every detail you need to come alive. And now my art is alive, and you are alive. It's time for me to bless you with my love and my greatest hopes."

> There is nothing more magical than the process of creation itself; in making art, you are giving shape to your breath, touch, and psyche.
>
> —LISA MARIE BASILE

Close your eyes and wait to feel the presence of the egregore. When you feel it, envision it before you. Pet it with love.

"The creative spirit and I have brought you into the world, and now we give you what you need to thrive. We bless you with the ability to inspire." Envision the egregore breathing the magickal air of the circle. "We give you our fiery passion and the will to be courageous." Touch the egregore's heart and envision fire leaping from your chest, traveling down your arms, and passing through your hands, into the heart of the egregore. "We give you hydration and serenity." Embrace the egregore. Feel your emotions well up within you and give that energy to it. "And we give you a body so perfect and beautiful, that you may live and thrive." Imagine that you can feel its body beneath your fingertips. Take a moment to make any last energetic adjustments to the egregore, such as smoothing its hide or adjusting its frequency. Bond with it, and in your mind's eye, see the creative spirit doing the same. When you're ready, release your embrace and gaze at it.

"Great spirit, you must be hungry. We have gifts for you—food and drink. Would you like some?" Make a big show of plating the food and offering it with humility. Serve its drink in a regal manner. Encourage the egregore to eat and drink, then engage with it more.

When you feel love in your heart for the egregore, say, "You were created by me and the creative spirit from a place of infinite love and curiosity. And as you grew and developed, we fell even more in love with you. You have earned our love and trust. It's with so much happiness that I give you these gifts."

Imagine that a golden light shines from your chest onto the egregore's chest. See it accept the light and become even more lively.

"May you bring joy, mystery, and wisdom to all who encounter you." Include any additional qualities you want your art to have. "May you be protected from all malevolent entities. May you slip through their grasp with the blessings and the protection of my guardians. May it be so!"

Ask the egregore if it's ready to meet the world. You should receive a positive answer and see its enthusiasm. (If you don't, ask questions until you get to the root of it, and then heal it with your affection.) You can continue to ask it questions, including what its name is. Alternately, you can start to close the ritual.

"Egregore, it's time for us to go, but before we do, we thank you for being so brave. We'll never forget that. When I close this circle, you can stay in my creative workplace, or you can go out into the world. If you go out, you can engage with others. I only ask that you visit me again."

Breathe in energy from the celestials and the guardians. Face the directions as you speak. "Thank you, element of earth and spirits of the north. Thank you, element of water and spirits of west. Thank you, element of fire and spirits of the south, and thank you, element of air and spirits of east. I release you, and I release the circle. The circle is open. Thank you, guardians, for protecting us in this ritual. Thank you, creative spirit. I appreciate you."

Take a moment to breathe in some of the remnant energy in the air until you feel yourself overflowing again. Then, ground your body by eating the food and drinking a beverage. It is done! Your egregore is now blessed and protected for whatever happens next.

Tips for Revision

- Continue to use the creative ritual to get in place to revise. Call upon the egregore to help you revise your project.

- If you have problems revising in the location where you created your art, change things up. A different atmosphere could inspire a different mindset and better work. Try working in silence or with different music.

- You may have different creative correspondences for revising. Be open to them. Review the correspondences for each chapter and try ones that interest you to see if they work.

- Consider using beta reviewers or a professional reviewer. They can give you information that can improve your art.

The Art of Finishing a Project

This is the finish line! Congratulations—you made it! You've crossed so much inner terrain. I can't underestimate how amazing this stage is. You turned an unseen dream into something that can be experienced by others. Take a moment to celebrate yourself and all your magickal, creative abilities.

CHAPTER 9

The Magician's Reveal: Releasing Your Art into the World

Now that you've finished your art, what do you want to do with it? There are so many options. You could go big or stay small. You can show it at a local place or post it online to the world (or both). You could give your art to friends or not tell a soul. Whatever you decide, one thing is certain—you must let your art go. It's done, so it's time to either put it away or send it out. It's understandable if you feel that you don't want to share your art. Some art is too personal for anyone else to see, and it's fine to keep those works to yourself. However, if you're uncertain or afraid of how it will be received, consider sharing it with someone you trust. Ask for constructive feedback. It's common for beginner artists to start with smaller audiences of people they trust before they consider putting their art out there to wider audiences. This process can help you build tougher skin and confidence as your art improves over time.

If you do choose to release your art to the world so others can enjoy it too, this chapter has some helpful tips. It was written to introduce the various ways to release art, as well as the joys and the turbulence that may come with the release. For the sake of this chapter, the words *perform* and *release* include actual performances, releases, publications, showings, parties, and events. They basically mean having your art in the public sphere, whether in person or online.

The Art of Performance

Magicians and witches send magick out to the world when they want to effect change. Artists also must send their creative work out and into the world so it can do its work. Whenever an artist releases their work into the world, they give some of their overflowing inspiration from the creative spirit to anyone who partakes in their art. It's almost like using a lit sparkler to light up a few other people's sparkers, who in turn light other people's sparklers, and so on, until the creative energy spreads far and wide. By the way, in this metaphor, a lit sparkler (inspiration) always returns to us, often in our darkest moments when we really need to see something beautiful. We always have several unlit sparklers in our pockets too, as they represent the potential to be inspired. Sharing inspiration is a unique kind of multiplication magick because the creative spirit only gave the passion (flame) to one person, but it became something far greater. Plato and Socrates believed that the muses created this kind of ripple effect, which lifts humanity and ultimately makes it better.[66] I agree. Performing well allows inspiration to be transmitted with ease, so it's worth considering. Good performers know that performing well is all about energy and presence. Fortunately, both of these vital qualities can be learned and improved over time.

---

66. Plato, *Essential Dialogues of Plato*, 11.

TRANSFORM FEAR INTO EXCITEMENT

Most people are afraid of going onto a stage and being the center of attention. One of the best things performing has taught me is how to change my fearful feelings into excitement. When it comes down to it, we experience fear in two different ways: as physical symptoms, or what we feel in our bodies, and as fearful thinking, which can conjure emotions.

The physical aspect of performing is part of our fight, flight, or freeze mechanism due to the burst of adrenaline most artists get before a performance. You might think that all my years of fire dancing would make me confident before performing, but I still get jitters. My heart quickens, and I feel thirsty, sweaty, hot, and cold at the same time. These are natural reactions, and I've learned to not interpret them as bad vibes. They're just what happens. It turns out there's a connection between pressure and creativity. The word *express* means to show artistic or creative abilities and also to use pressure to squeeze something out.[67] This can be a good thing if it helps performers give their best to the audience.

The first thing you need to know about turning your jitters into empowerment is that fearful sensations have the same feelings as those of excitement. They're both processed in the same area of the brain.[68] Instead of viewing these sensations as fearful reactions, you can recall how much you wanted to do the performance and how much you want to share your vision with other people. You can take a few deep breaths, and it's as if a switch is

---

67. *Merriam-Webster*, s.v. "express (*v.*)," accessed October 17, 2022, https://www.merriam-webster.com/dictionary/express.

68. Alex Korb, "Predictable Fear: Why the Brain Likes Haunted Houses," *Psychology Today*, October 31, 2014, https://www.psychologytoday.com/us/blog/prefrontal-nudity/201410/predictable-fear.

flipped in your mind. This can help you no longer dread the performance and resist it, but instead view it as if you're lucky you get to do it. It frees up all that bound energy and fills you with a surge of energy to perform.

Taming the fearful mind is another beast. In situations like those, our minds often lie to us about what's happening. If you were to ask your mind what will happen, it'll probably tell you all the worst-case scenarios. You can talk back to it. Tell your mind it's highly unlikely that you'll die when you perform. Say it's unlikely that you'll trip and fall. Tell it you know your lines, and you've practiced them several times. The mind wants attention when it's trying to prevent something bad from happening. It interprets the performance as something bad. I've found it's helpful to think of the fearful mind like a pet that is only partially domesticated. When it's time to perform, it's like a heavy knock at the door. Your mind will either want to run and hide like a cat or bark like a dog. Neither of those animals is answering the door. The best thing you can do with a fearful mind is let your training kick in. Keep the energy you want for the performance and don't let the mind distract you. Ignore your pets and the nervous mind, compose yourself, and answer the door.

STAGE PRESENCE

Seasoned actors, dancers, and other performance artists have a certain kind of charm or gravity that is known as stage presence. It's as if they snap into character as soon as they're on stage. It usually has a certain posture or mannerism about it, and it's definitely magickal. Some people are gifted with a natural ability to show up in this way, but most people learn it through rituals. It's all about getting yourself into the right state of mind for the performance.

When you're in the rehearsal stage of your performance, develop a pre-performance ritual that brings out the right emotion or mentality. Music often helps us dial in to the right energetic state. If you find a song that puts you in that space, use it, and don't listen to it for any other purpose. Other people may want to try using aromas or reciting an intention. When you find the right mindset, take it with you on stage. Then, it's all about maintaining the presence for as long as you can without breaking authenticity or character.

It's helpful to anticipate what could take you out of your stage presence and the solutions you'd take. For instance, if looking at another performer always throws you off because of how funny they are, try not looking directly at them. If a certain part makes you uncomfortable, find a way to turn your discomfort into a power. You can't control what happens at every performance, but by practicing stage performance, you'll improve every time.

Egotism versus Performing Well

You've probably seen someone perform with their ego on display. Unless this is used farcically, these kinds of performances are dull and uninspiring. An egotistical performer rarely transmits any energy to their audience because they cycle it back toward themselves to feed their sense of lack. By doing this, they don't give anyone a sense of who they are. It's like they're hiding behind a facade. This kind of front takes a lot of energy to maintain—to do so, they must try to absorb all the energy in the room. They direct the flow of their performance back toward themselves instead of letting the energy flow through them and into the audience. If you've been there, don't feel bad. A lot of performers go through a stage like this, especially when they were first starting out. There's such a huge learning curve about performing, and information about how to perform isn't readily available. Even advanced performers fall into this state when they can't reveal what they're truly feeling. This is yet another reason why it's so important to have a balanced life whenever possible, including managing your stress and mental health.

You can avoid egotistic performances by giving your energy to your audience. Performances are a gift of your authenticity, so be who you really are. That's who the audience wants to see. Actors even use this when they perform as characters—they insert some of their own vulnerability into the character. Skip the facade. Let your soul show up and allow the art to move through you. Good performances display your confidence, your ability to be in your body, and your courage to share your vision. Even if you only show one of these aspects, the performance will likely be successful. The audience will feel it deep in their bones, and they'll appreciate you for it.

ENERGY LADDERS

One of the best tricks for performing well is something I call *energy ladders*. In performances, it's when a performer accepts energy from the audience and transmits their performance even stronger. This in turn feeds the audience, who gives the energy back to the performer. This concept explains how great performers can uplift an entire stadium of people. If you're a performer, get comfortable with the concept of exchanging energy with your audience. Anyone who is paying attention to your performance is exchanging energy with you on one level or another. Accept their reactions and allow them to inform your response to them. Build the energy. This theory is clear in improvisation acting classes such as those at the Second City, who teach their pupils to say, "yes and ..." When you accept what's happening, you can build bridges between yourself and the audience. You can also use this exchange to inform the direction and correct your course. Accept their energy and give it back to them through your art. Play with the flow of energy and be brave enough to enhance it with your personal flavor.

Performance Spirits

Spirits can enhance performances, and they're worth utilizing if you're open to it. Artists can use the egregore of their art to step into a more powerful conveyance of it. The performance can become especially powerful when the artist taps into a greater egregore that's in accordance with the artist's vision. For example, an actor in a new play can portray their character while also using inspiration from other, well-known characters to make their performance stronger. Or the egregore of a certain quality can be used, such as the egregore of serenity or greed. This energy is known by everyone, and they're relatively easy to tap into. When this happens, the actor can easily step into more powerful expressions because of the power of those well-known egregores. They give a defining energy to the performance.

Another performance spirit is the duende, which you may recall from chapter 1. It's known for inciting powerful performances that move audiences emotionally. It can evoke a variety of feelings, including cleverness, sensuality, joy, brooding, and wrath. It's hard to describe duende because it's both of this world and not of this world, but you know it when you see it. It looks and feels like an overflowing aura, a torrent of energy, or a feeling of the supernatural. Sometimes, the people who witness it experience a profound healing. The duende can't be ordered to come for a performance. It only comes when the artist feels authentic and deep emotions. This is likely the reason why actors and musicians are told to use their emotions in their art—because it invites the duende to show up. This may also be the star quality that performers aspire to have.

One stunning example of star quality is the gravity and charm that the actress Marilyn Monroe had. There is a rumor she could turn her star power off and on, even while walking anonymously on busy New York streets with a friend. Monroe supposedly asked her friend, "Do you want to see me become her?" Her friend said yes, and she was amazed to see Monroe transform before her eyes. "She turned something on within herself that was almost like magic. And suddenly, cars were slowing, and people were turning their heads and stopping to stare.... [It was] as if she pulled off a mask or something, even though a second ago, nobody noticed her."[69]

Monroe had a lot of emotion to draw from, including childhood trauma, lifelong nightmares, insomnia, bipolar disorder, painful endometriosis, learning disorders, and a drug problem. For artists with intense emotions, like Monroe, giving performances with the duende can give them an extremely beneficial outlet for that energy. However, the need to repeat the same performance can create issues because the duende doesn't always come when artists call upon it. It doesn't like schedules, and two shows with duende may be very different because the emotions they express are different. Like the creative spirit, you can only create the right conditions for it to come.

Performance spirits can possess artists, to one degree or another. Musicians especially talk about experiences of chan-

69. Edie Weinstein, "The Marilyn Monroe Effect: The Nonverbal Communication of Confidence," Psych Central, last modified September 2, 2019, https://psychcentral.com/blog/the-marilyn-monroe-effect-the-nonverbal-communication-of-confidence.

neling spirits and deities who perform through them. Wendy Rule, a witch musician who gives Full Moon Magic concerts, said, "I often feel that I am a channel for these energies [spirits and deities]. I open up and let them flow through me....At other times, I feel more like I am witnessing and holding space for these powerful beings."[70] Sharing the stage with the performance spirit likely helps the artist perform to the best of their ability and give a moving concert.

Similarly, when talking about performing, Tori Amos said, "Morphing into...channeling Tori who is going to channel the songs...I leave the mother and the wife, that side of me, back in the dressing room, to the point where my husband will pass me in the hallway and say, you know, 'I want my wife back when you're done, boss....' And I will say as I'm morphing, 'You will have your wife back. She's safe. She's where she needs to be.'"[71] In this case, the artist is still present, but their day-to-day concerns are replaced by something larger than they are, which helps them perform.

> There is transformative magic present in both the creative artistic process and the participatory act of observing an artistic creation.
>
> —S. ELIZABETH

70. Kelden, "The Magic of Persephone: An Interview with Wendy Rule," *By Athame and Stang* (blog), Patheos, July 9, 2019, https://www.patheos.com /blogs/byathameandstang/2019/07/persephone-wendy-rule/.

71. Pam Shaffer, "Ep 95: Tori Amos." October 27, 2021, in *Why Not Both,* produced by Laura Studarus and *Under the Radar* magazine, podcast, MP3 audio, 14:27–15:02, https://anchor.fm/why-not-both/episodes /Ep-95-Tori-Amos-e198uoj.

Yet another option is to ask a deity or a specific spirit to influence your performance. Ideally, this relationship would begin during practice sessions, and you'll have a shared goal for the performance. These spirits or divinities can get you into the right mindset and enhance your performance with their various aspects, especially if you get nervous.

For improvisation artists, the creative spirit and the performance spirit are often one and the same. This super-altered state gives the audience even more energy. However, I assume most artists work with one spirit for the creation process and the other for the performance. A large part of this depends on your art format, your creative process, and your artistic persona.

• Exercise •
EVOKING THE DUENDE AND THE CREATIVE SPIRIT

For some people, the process of evoking a duende and grounding it into their body is effortless. For others, these steps will prove helpful. Any artist can bring about duende in a performance as long as their emotions are genuine and they can navigate trance states. It's worth noting that the duende doesn't give artists talent—rather, it's a passionate expression of the existing talent. The more advanced they are, the more of an artistic experience it will be, but even beginners can find something worthwhile in this exercise. This exercise will be especially helpful for stage artists such as dancers, actors, and musicians. Anyone can benefit from the relationship, though, and you never know when you might want to use it.

Set aside about thirty minutes to an hour in your creative space for this exercise. The only materials you need are a mirror and music. Ideally, the music should bring your mind into a trance state. Try droning music, rhythmic drumming, or ambient sounds. For your first time, use emotionally neutral music so the energy of the duende won't be confused with that of the music. Afterward, when you've established a sense of what the duende feels like, you can play any kind of music that makes you feel passionate or emotional.

Before you start, cleanse the space and add protection to it. For example, you can cast a circle or ask your deities or guides to protect you from all spirits except for your creative spirit and the duende. Dim the lights. Do the steps of the creative ritual and get your mind into the right state to contact the creative spirit. As your mind shifts, do a few gentle warm-up stretches to ground into your body.

The first step to evoke the duende is to set an intention to do so. You may say something like, "I invite the duende into this room. If it feels right for both of us, I'll welcome the duende into my body, but for no longer than five minutes. If I request it to leave, it must leave." Feel free to change this intention as you see fit—it's a more conservative statement for beginners, so they can ease into the experience without being overwhelmed.

Next, take a few deep breaths and sway your body back and forth. Allow the music to guide your movements. Slowly lower yourself to the floor and lie down on your back or on your side. Think of a strong emotion from the depths of your being. It should be something you feel secure about sharing with these spirits and not something that will reopen a traumatic wound. Choose whatever emotion you can dismiss if you need to. Let your feeling come out of the depths and spread until you feel it in your entire body, from the tips of your toes to the top of your head, to your fingertips, and on the surface of your skin. Continue breathing deeply and feeling, and start to move intuitively until you enter a trance state in which ordinary time has no hold on you. It may take twenty minutes or longer to reach this point.

When you feel your mind slip into the trance state, stand up while retaining any movements and breathing patterns that help you keep the trance state. Be aware of the duende in the room with you. Sense what this spirit feels like. Is it playful, fun, and lively, or does it have an emotional depth that's more akin to sorrow, anger, or madness? Mentally ask the duende whether it means you harm or not. If you receive an answer that it does not wish you any harm, say something like, "Duende, I invite you and only you into my body for the next five (or ten or thirty) minutes, but you must be gentle with my body. If I say you must leave, you must go immediately. Do you agree?" If you receive confirmation, proceed. If you don't receive confirmation, ask again. If you still don't receive a favorable answer, banish the spirit and utilize more protection in your creative space before trying again.

Move your body with the influence of the duende. Let go of some control over your body and find your way with it as you move together. The spirit may inhabit you by incremental degrees or by a greater magnitude. Find the right give and take. The right exchange of energy will feel like an empowering trance that compels you to keep moving. When you feel a comfortable mixture between yourself and the duende, breathe deeply into that strong emotion. Allow the emotion to overtake you—let that feeling and the duende rise to the surface of your skin. The duende feeds on this feeling, so feed it well. Allow the duende to extend its energy into your limbs. Your movements don't have to be complicated or artful at this point. Whatever feels natural for the emotion is fine. You can close your eyes completely to get more lost in the feeling, or you can open them slightly to be more aware of your surroundings.

Look at the mirror so you can see your reflection, but don't gaze directly into your own eyes. Instead, imagine the person in the reflection is your audience. Ask the duende to help you tell the story of the emotion to the audience. Feel the depths of your emotion again (as deep as is comfortably possible) and let the duende give it life.

At this point, you can try your hand at dance, acting, music, or poetry. It can be a practiced piece or impromptu. Let the duende change things according to the flow of emotion. With each movement or word, allow the feeling to become more intense. Direct your performance to the audience and send all your energy there. Play with the levels of your emotional expression. Try giving the audience 100 percent of the emotion and see what that feels like and looks like. Then, keep the emotion very present within you, but only show 80 percent of it. It may help to imagine a veil is covering you. Even when your emotion is partially hidden, its power should remain very present. When you've reached that level, take the expression down to 50 percent and then 20 percent. Try to remember what these different percentages look like so you can think about using them in choreography. They can also be used when you need to conserve your energy.

You can curtail the session whenever you like. A beginner will likely not get this far on their first try, and that's completely fine. Usually, when you start to feel tired or you know the spirit is leaving, it's a good idea to call it a session. With practice, you'll be able to maintain the interaction for longer periods. Sit down with your spine supported or lay down. Say something like, "Duende, thank you for showing me these new ways of expression. I appreciate your insights and I enjoyed this. I hope we can do it again sometime soon. I release you from my body, and I ask you to leave this

space now so I can rest and process this experience. Thank you."
Recover with water, food, and rest.

• *Meditation* •
ENVISION YOUR PERFORMANCE

Professional athletes, performers, and speakers all have one thing in common: they envision their work in the world before they do it. It helps them create focus and channel more success, even when the pressure is on. This meditation about your performance can help you find the best energetic pathway as well. It takes about fifteen minutes. For the best results, rewrite it to apply to your performance and record it. Listen to it anytime you feel fearful of performing.

Sit or lie down somewhere comfortable. Take a few deep breaths. With every inhalation, allow your body to feel a little lighter. Imagine you're getting ready for your performance. Picture yourself doing what needs to be done to get completely ready. When you're ready, take a moment to look at yourself in a mirror and smile. See the most confident version of yourself reflected at you. Take another deep breath that expands the belly and release any tension you may feel. As you look at yourself in the mirror again, see how ready you are for the performance.

Now, fast forward to seeing yourself at the place you'll be performing. You're there, and in just one moment, you'll start. How do you feel? If you feel fear, know that it's just a feeling of excitement for the performance. Take another deep breath and feel a sense of clarity and ease sweep through you. And now, it's time for the performance. Envision yourself going out to perform. You're having fun and looking wonderful. You can call upon the duende or your creative spirit if you wish. You might see yourself exchanging a bit of energy with the audience. Go through all the actions of your performance with confidence. Have fun with it and show that feeling to everyone there. Receive the energy from the audience and give it back to them through your show.

When your performance is over, envision yourself taking a bow or waving if that's appropriate, and leaving the stage. Rest for a moment and savor the sweetness of a great performance. Say something affirmative to yourself, such as "I nailed it" or "I knocked it out of the park!" Hold this feeling—allow yourself to feel it deep in your bones. Take another deep breath and give yourself a bit of gratitude. Give gratitude to the spirit(s) as well if you called upon them. Take an energizing breath and wiggle your toes. Feel your imagination return to your body. Run your hands over your arms to ground you in the present moment.

• Ritual •
BLESS YOUR PERFORMANCE OR RELEASE

This ritual can be used to magickally send off your creation and celebrate your accomplishment. It can be big and public or small and private. It may not be appropriate for all artists, so make any variations you need to personalize it for your needs.

Materials
table or another altar space
altar cloth
your art or a representation of it
your creative correspondences for air (incense, oils, music)
your creative correspondences for earth (herbs, crystals)
cupcakes or sheet cake
candles

lighter or matches
fancy beverage such as sparkling wine
fancy glass
additional glasses, plates, forks, knife for cutting cake (optional)

Set up an altar with a cloth and your art. Play the music that you used for creativity or something that makes you feel happy. Light the incense or anoint yourself with the oil. Lovingly set up the cake and the candles on the table. When you feel excitement about this stage of your project, activate your creative potential within you and light the candles. Next, pour the beverage and drink deeply. Relish every drop. You can dance if you wish.

When you feel your energy lift a little, refill your glass if necessary and raise it to thank the creative spirit and the egregore of your project and toast them. If you're in mixed company and you don't want to toast the spirits, simply give a toast to your art. A good toast for this kind of celebration would have a personal statement of who you were before you ever thought about creating, a little bit about the inspiration that came to you, mention of a few adversities you overcame, and an acknowledgment of the product and everyone in attendance. End the toast with a raised glass and a phrase such as *cheers* or *Here's to* _____! Clink glasses with someone nearby. Of course, you can use the egregore of your art to give your toast more energy, if you wish, but only if you've experienced it and you're comfortable bringing it out in front of others.

Get some cake, and as you eat, imagine that the egregore and your creative spirit are with you, enjoying the event. Leave a little bit of cake on your plate for the egregore to eat. When it's time to clean up, extinguish the candles and collect your items. They have been charged up from the event, and as long as the energy they carry is supportive, they'll be even more powerful in your creative rituals in the future. Thank the egregore and the creative spirit once again and take the good energy home with you.

Tips for Releasing Your Art

- Practice your performance until you're comfortable with it. Practice it with people watching too so you get an idea of what it'll be like.

- Look at the performance space a few weeks before the event begins. Knowing the layout will help you feel more secure about your performance.

- Tell people about your performance or art show. Call, message, and email people. Print flyers and create a graphic. Make an online event and alert the news. Ask a couple of friends to take photos or videos.

- If you want to learn stage presence and build a thicker skin, take a course on improvisational speaking.

- Before you perform, find your center. Feel it in your body. Flip your fear into excitement.

- Don't worry about mistakes at this point. Everyone has them. People will give you the benefit of the doubt.

Release Your Art with Joy

I hope you have fun with your performance or art release. If possible, celebrate this moment to enjoy it all the more and to mark how far you've come. It takes courage to put yourself out there. Never underestimate the ability of your art to affect someone in a fabulous way. Your art is a gift to the people who are receptive to it.

CHAPTER 10

Post-Release: Liminal Rest, Recharge, and Reflection

Life keeps moving. After a big release of your art and all the events that go with it, attention inevitably turns away from your project. As the initial thrill settles down, it's replaced by different energy—that of rest and recharge. I believe you should lean into the liminal time between creative projects. There's a mystical, recharging energy that can only be found in the lulls. It's one of the greatest tools of creativity, and it can give you so much inspiration for your next creative venture. Although this chapter isn't very magickal, it is part of a healthy artistic cycle. After the harvest, the fallow season arrives. It may seem that the earth is cold and barren during winter, but there's a purpose to it. Only the hardiest of seeds will make it to the next season, which will make the next growing season more productive and successful. This time of change is a pivotal moment for your art. Use the liminal energy that naturally arises to make sustainable changes to your life and your art.

After the Release

When you finally finish a project, a lot of emotions can come up. You may feel exhausted if it was a particularly big project or if you extended a lot of energy toward it. I hope you find joy in your journey. One of the most important things you can do at this stage is to allow yourself to feel pride and contentment. You undertook a huge journey, and you made it to the end! A lot of people don't make it that far. At this stage, a lot of artists fixate on their next goal without letting their accomplishments sink in. This tendency comes from our workaholic culture, which always asks, "What's next?" Letting the culture of business dictate the terms of your creativity is a huge mistake. Remember, art is bigger than your accomplishments, and the endpoint is only a small part of the story. Take a moment to pause. Art changes artists. You deserve to let those changes sink in before rushing into the next project. Give yourself space to figure out who you are now, what you like, and which ways you want to express yourself.

RECAP

While your art is fresh in your mind, think about everything you did. What worked well? What didn't work at all? Is there anything you'd change? Evaluate your performance with compassion and take notes in your creative notebook. If you don't know the answers, simply begin writing and see if you come to any realizations. Review these pages when it comes time to create again.

CRITICS: CONSIDER THE SOURCE

You'll inevitably run into critiques of your art. In my experience, there's a bell curve of reactions for every art. Some people will never like anything you do, and others will love everything. Most people will be in the middle. You have little control over how others perceive your art, and the most important reception is your own. As long as you like your art and you don't let other people's criticisms become your own thoughts, you'll be fine.

With that, there are a few things to keep in mind when dealing with critics.

Remember that critics are critiquing your art, not you. Never make someone's rejection of your art into a rejection of you. Their reaction is to your art, and it's not about you. It's about them, what they've been taught, and what they prefer at this time. That's why there are usually over thirty different kinds of ice cream in a supermarket—because not everyone likes the same thing. Maybe you love chocolate ice cream, but another person only likes fruit sorbets. Your chocolate ice cream will never be a sorbet, no matter how much you try to make it so. Can you live with your chocolate ice cream, knowing you love it and you don't have to please everyone? I hope so. I hope you don't try to make sorbet. That person will find their sorbet, and you'll attract other people who also love chocolate ice cream. Who knows—over time, the person who said they didn't like chocolate ice cream may change their mind, and they may be a fan after all. Keeping an open mind helps you not care as much about what they think.

When someone gives you feedback, consider whether that person deserves to be listened to or not. How do you feel about that person? If you don't like them, feel free to disregard their response. You probably don't have a lot in common, and they're probably not the ideal audience for it. If someone really doesn't get along with you, if there's a fundamental difference in the way you are, the way you communicate, or what you believe, take their feedback with a whole shaker of salt. Another question to ask yourself is whether the critic has undertaken a creative journey or not. Have they produced something, and do they know what it's like to put everything into a project and put it out there in the world? Too often, people who are scared to create try to knock others down to make themselves feel better. If they haven't created anything and their critique is excessively harsh, don't listen to it.

Please also don't be fooled by anyone who brings up concepts of "real art" or "good and bad art." Those critiques speak a lot more about how much of a perfectionist they are rather than what kind of artist you are. Whatever you create is real art. Be aware of high bars and people who set them, and don't hold yourself to their standards of perfection. Your art does not have to be in a museum or shown on Broadway to be real art. If that were the case, most artists wouldn't be considered real artists. Some people just like to argue and complain, and you have a choice in whether or not you listen to them.

One of the most powerful messages I've read about criticism is that artists are seldom hurt by the truth.[72] In other words, most artists are self-aware enough to shrug about their faults. They know what they're working on, and they can admit it. Those critiques don't sting. It's the exaggerated falsehoods that hurt the most and keep people from creating again. Be aware of any exaggerations and write them off. Don't let them enter your narrative about your art.

If critics bring up fearful sensations in you, you're not alone. Most people feel that way about being critiqued. The funny thing about fear is that it's never vanquished by mastering every technique and skill. It can only be conquered by growing larger than it, just as you did when you turned fear into excitement. Fear will only dissipate when you feel proud of yourself for expressing your authenticity. With repeated releases, you'll gain thicker skin. Even if someone does try to make their critique personal, ask yourself whether you'd rather be authentic or popular. Authentic-

---

72. Cameron and Bryan, *The Artist's Way*, 130.

ity runs a lot deeper than popularity, which waxes and wanes. It's far easier to please yourself than the masses because their tastes change all the time. Always be authentic in your art. Don't ever make art for your critics. Make it for yourself. A critic's opinion is never as important as your own.

AVOIDING POST-RELEASE BLUES

Some people, myself included, have felt a bit down after releasing a creation into the world. The moment of releasing your art can feel like a thunderstorm of energy with electricity running through you. This wild pendulum swing equals out, which often makes the ensuing quietude that much more deafening. A similar thing happens to some magickal practitioners after a big ritual—they complain of feeling depleted or drained. There are two general ways to deal with energy depletion after a ritual or a release. The first is to rest up, ground into your body, eat some delicious food, and drink something hydrating (more about that in a bit). The other method of replenishing energy is more interesting and advanced. After releasing your work, absorb the energy of your accomplishment. With deep breaths, drink the energy in. Receive the appreciation, applause, compliments, and congratulations by taking them into your energetic field. If you feel the blues, recall that moment and mentally accept your successes. (This is a variation of a post-ritual energy replenishment method taught by Laura Tempest Zakroff, dancer and author of witchcraft books such as *Sigil Witchery* and *Weaving the Liminal*.) For some people, the post-release blues may be an inevitable part of the creation cycle, and nothing will equalize the situation. If this sounds like you, don't be too hard on yourself. You accomplished a lot. Keep reading for ideas and activities to keep you feeling sustained.

Rest and Recharge

It's likely that your creative project took a lot out of you. Even if you tried to attain balance, you may have put too many hours in. Now that your project is over, give yourself a moment to stop creating and simply rest up. Enjoy the freedom from creating. As much as I love being creative, I also believe it's so good to take a break from it. I suggest breaking right after your project is complete and taking advantage of your free time. The days can feel longer, and with all the time on your hands, the world can seem fresh and new. You may even have energy now. What will you do with all this free time and energy? Here are some suggestions.

DECOMPRESS

Resting is wonderful, but if you can do something soul-renewing, do it. Here's a hint—it's not work. Joyful events, where you can get away from it all, can really help you release the project from your system and find yourself again. Book a vacation, buy tickets to concerts, camp, or go to a festival. You could visit a natural wonder like the ocean, walk through ancient caverns, or explore the paths of an old-growth forest. Look for events that allow you to feel as free as possible. A change of scenery is an added bonus—it does wonders for the mind and the soul. Even if you can only take a couple of days off, it'll likely change you in multiple beneficial ways.

CATCH UP

With all your extra time, you now have a chance to catch up on the things you've been putting off for a while. Use your break to accomplish the things you've been wanting to do. You might want to see the movies that came out or visit family. Maybe you'll see friends or read a book you've had your eye on for a while. Reading fiction will also let you decompress because interesting characters can often trigger our own thoughts about how we relate to the world. Hold off on repairs for now. Anything that feels like work won't give you the sensation you're looking for.

CONTINUE TO CELEBRATE

Be sure to celebrate your accomplishments again. You deserve to feel a sense of pride in what you've done. Don't let your release feel like a one-and-done kind of thing. Celebrate when the one-month mark comes around. Do it again at the three-month mark, and the six-month, and the first anniversary. Eat something fancy and drink something nice. Celebrate the project and yourself.

DO THE OPPOSITE OF YOUR ART

Now is a great time to practice the opposite of your art. In creativity, doing the opposite of what you did will help you rebalance your life and fill in the experiences you missed out on. It can also let you consider new projects for the next time you do create. For example, performers can look inward as opposed to projecting their art outward. Dancers may want to read more books and let their bodies rest. A carver could let their hands rest up and listen to more music instead.

By doing the opposite, these artists open themselves to worlds that had been restricted before. The goal of this activity is to enjoy the pleasure of the opposites and be in the present moment. It gives us true rest from our art, and the ability to banish burnout.

TRY SOMETHING NEW

New experiences are favored at this time. It's significant to note that at this point of change, you're not tied to any art goals. This means you can pivot and go in multiple directions. What have you always wanted to learn how to do? Exploring other arts expands our abilities and our mental capacities.

GET BORED

One of the ways to be more creative is to get bored. Do all the things you wanted to do, and then do absolutely nothing. You'd be amazed by what a little space can give you. It's almost as if the mind becomes quieter, and you can hear yourself better. Getting to this point has given me objectivity and a still point from which I can go anywhere. It refreshes my mind and gives me objectivity about what's working and what isn't. For me, this feeling sinks in about three to four weeks after turning in a big project. I believe boredom is the secret to coming up with the next great thing. Often, it's a sustainable way to produce good material.

CONSIDER CHARITY

If you have time and resources to show your art for a charity or a non-profit organization you believe in, do it. Those events are enlivening, especially when you're surrounded by other people who care about the same cause as you do. You'll get to network with a lot of people, and the new friends you make there will give you a better sense of community.

CREATE A BUSINESS

If you're good at your art and you can charge money for it, consider selling your products. There are many benefits to this, including getting your art before more people and paying some of your material costs and studio bills. Research the market to see what other people charge for similar work and price your art at your talent level. This can open more doors such as networking, creative partnerships, and opportunities for commissions. However, your creative projects don't have to become your main source of income. When you depend on your art for your living, you may fall into the trap of producing things that you don't love simply because they sell, which could make you love your art less. Remember to always do what you love and be true to yourself, first and foremost.

• Ritual •
RESTORATIVE BATH

Salt baths are refreshing and cleansing. They're a sublime magickal practice for fallow times when rest is of the utmost importance because they incorporate relaxation. This restorative bath ritual uses a "second bath," or a mug of bath water, for the creative spirit to enjoy. The mug doesn't have to be fancy, but you should choose one that your creative spirit likes or one that you used when you made your art. Move slowly for this ritual. All your actions for this ritual should be serene and unhurried so you can absorb the restful energy.

If you don't have a prepared dilution of lavender oil in a carrier oil, make your own by mixing one drop of lavender oil to thirty drops of carrier oil on a saucer. You'll only need to use about a quarter of the oil for the ritual. The rest can be used to massage your muscles or feet.

Materials
relaxing music
5 drops of diluted lavender oil
cleansed white chime candle or a white pillar candle
candleholder
lighter
2 handfuls of Epsom salts
1 tablespoon of baking soda
mug

Play the relaxing music and start to run the bathwater. Rub the oil into your hands and thank them for all the wonderful work they did. Inhale the calming aroma of lavender, and allow the feeling to sink into your body, mind, and spirit. While your hands are still oily, pick up the candle and hold it in your hands. Instill some of your peaceful feelings into it by allowing your emotion to flow from your hands and into the candle. Retain this feeling and spread the oil onto the candle with your fingertips until the entire candle is covered in oil. Place the candle in the candleholder and rinse the oil from your hands with the bathwater. Adjust the temperature of the water if necessary.

Take a moment to think about how rest is such a necessary part of the creative cycle. Daydream about what rest looks like for you. What do you see yourself doing to enjoy rest? Do any activities or ideas come to mind? How can you honor this natural part of the cycle?

When you're ready to go deeper, think about activating your creative potential for the purposes of rest, and light the candle. Enjoy its light and feel how you can be an artist even when you're not actively creating. Place the candle somewhere safe nearby.

Sprinkle the salt and the baking soda into the bathwater and place the mug near the bathtub so it's within reach. In your own time, step into the bathwater and sink deep into the waters. Get the mug and scoop a mugful of bathwater out. Say, "This is for you, creative spirit. May this resting time be good for both of us." Set the mug down nearby. Breathe deeply and allow any tension you have to melt away.

When you feel settled in the tub, think of your creative spirit and your most recent art project. Recall how you felt when you first started it, and then throughout making the rough draft, the revision process, and finishing it. You've been on quite a journey! Think about the egregore of your art and the release or performance, if that's applicable. Remember the celebrations you held for it. With the next exhalation, send sweet energy to the egregore and bless the project in your own way.

Continue to breathe deeply. With every exhalation, release the energy of your project from your mind and body so you can fully move into the resting period. Let it go. Release any tension you're holding in your muscles. Close your eyes and feel the mellow lull. Rest. There's beauty in being still. Find it and feel it.

When you feel nearly ready to leave the bath, envision yourself doing the restorative activities you identified earlier. Make a commitment to do one of them in the coming week.

Say, "Thank you, creative spirit. I'll call upon you again when I'm ready for our next project." Pour the mug of bathwater back into the bath. Blow out the candle.

Step out of the bathtub, again being mindful to use slow movements. Towel off and enjoy your rest and relaxation time. Use the candle again whenever you want to feel more restful.

Check In with the Egregore

An easy way to reconnect with your egregore is to take five minutes to lie down and think about it. When you see it in your mind, notice how it has changed. What does it look like now? Observe it, interact with it, and note how friendly or standoffish it is. What other description words come to mind? What colors is it? Notice how it makes you feel and what size it is. Give it a little energy and affection. Give it more energy and watch it grow. You can converse with it if you wish. Asking it questions will tell you a lot about how it's changing over time and with other people's perceptions. When you're ready, tell it you'll see it later and give it one last bit of affection. Record your experience in your journal or Book of Shadows.

Tips for Future Projects

- When the creative spirit whispers to you again, take notes but don't act on them until you've rested up sufficiently. If it insists, tell it how much more time you need.
- Follow your bliss. Your next project should be deeply interesting to you.
- Your next project is allowed to be different from the last one. You don't have to make a sequel or only have minor variations. You're constantly evolving, so your art should be too.
- Rewrite your artist's vision statement with your new sense of self. You've changed a lot since the last project, and this will show you what's most important now.
- Learn more, organize more, practice more, and revise more, but work smarter, not harder. Cut out unnecessary

duties and time-wasting tasks. Get to the heart of the matter faster.

- As you improve as an artist, bless your old creations and your early works of art. They were the best you could do at the time, and they showed you the path to being an artist.

- When you're ready to begin your next project, do so with intention.

- You may not need all the steps of the creative ritual. After I found my artist's path to the flow, I reduced the creative correspondences to only the ones I needed. With that being said, if you're in a pinch, use your old correspondences to bring on the flow. They can really give you a big boost when you need it the most.

Completing the Larger Cycle

There is magick in making art, but there's also magick in *not* making art. Taking a break can be a big change. Be sure to give yourself plenty of flexibility so you can adjust with grace. Rest, decompress, and find your joy.

Art Life

Thank you for taking this journey with me to explore the magick of making art with the creative spirit. Art life is utterly magickal, and artists who engage with their creative spirits belong to an extraordinary group. As with magickal practitioners, there's a certain kind of mystery about them that can only come from art magick and communicating with the other side. Those inner journeys leave tracks, which can be sensed in the depths and the heights of an artist's expressions. If you've met your creative spirit and you've made something together, I welcome you to this group. If you have yet to encounter it, I encourage you to keep trying. You'll find it if you keep at it.

Wherever you are on your creative journey, I hope you know that the creative spirit will knock on your mental door, again and again, with a bouquet of fresh ideas picked just for you. You may not sense it until you're deep into your process, but it'll happen. When it comes, be ready. Open the door and set the stage. Trust your artistic visions. Be brave enough to ignite your creative potential. Find your flow and do that good, hard work that yields such wonderful results. You have the magick of creativity deep in your bones. It's the path all our ancestors have walked, and it's yours for the finding too. May it be a blessing for you and the world.

Sincerely, Astrea

Acknowledgments

I have a lot of people to thank for assisting me with the writing of this book. First, I thank my husband, Tim, for our fabulous Rest Squad moments and for being my biggest creative supporter. I love how we have each other's backs through all kinds of blocks and successes. Thanks to Scarlett for bringing out your duende, for being my ride-or-die most of the time, for evolving along with me, and for sharing some of the most inspirational moments of my life. A big thanks to Jason Mankey for sharing resources and for all the therapeutic writer talk. I love talking with someone who is equally as obsessed with exploring ideas through writing. Thanks to Heather Greene for making my books better, and thanks to Markus Ironwood, Andrea Neff, Elysia Gallo, Lauryn Heineman, and the other wonderful people at Llewellyn for all they do.

I also thank the magickal people in my wider creative circles for camaraderie through the writing process—Laura, Tatiara, Scarlett, Heron, Phoenix, Meg, Ra, Tenae, Hana, Carla, and Mandi. Thanks to my wonderful friends Mary, Andrea, Ashes, Ali, Christine, T, and L. Thanks to Mark and Andrea, my amazing mentors, who not only turned on the lights but showed me where the light switch is located. I thank my family for being so awesome and for literally going extra miles to work around my writing schedule.

I deeply thank Liz Gilbert for writing *Big Magic* and for reintroducing the concept of the creative spirit to the world. That book really is magickal, and it inspired me to discover more personal gnosis that informed many parts of this book. Last, thanks to the local Metro Libraries, WYSO, and the podcast *Your Creative Push* for all the support over the years.

Deities Associated with Art and Creativity

Over the ages, there have been many deities associated with art. This section has several notable examples; however, the entries in this section are limited to their artistic aspects only. Absent from this list are the deities associated with fertility and the creation of the universe, as that kind of creativity isn't directly related to art. Deities of beauty, such as Aphrodite, Venus, and Freya are also omitted because, often, their beauty was considered a natural quality and not a talent. If you don't see your favorite creative deity here, they may not have been known for these aspects historically, but they can still inspire you to create. Use personal gnosis to interact with them.

If you're interested in any of these gods, learn more about them. Look for books that are primary sources or books that have primary sources in the bibliography. Interact with these deities individually for a while to get to know them before you engage them for creative assistance.

Apollo: Greek god of music and poetry

Arachne: Accomplished Greek weaver (although not a goddess)

Athena: Greek goddess of the arts

Bragi: Norse god of poetry, songs, and music

Brigid: Celtic goddess of poetry, metalwork, creativity, and inspiration

Cerridwen: Celtic goddess of poetry, songs, and keeper of the cauldron of awen (inspiration)

Dionysus: Greek god of dance, theater, and acting

Frigg: Norse goddess of creative arts

Hathor: Egyptian goddess of dance and music

Hephaestus: Greek god of artisans, including blacksmiths, carpenters, potters, and metalworkers

Hermes: Greek god of writing and communication

Khnemu: Egyptian god of pottery and ceramics

Lugh: Celtic god of craftsmanship and skill

Matangi: Hindu goddess of poetry and arts, especially for outcasts

Mercury: Roman god of writing and communication

Meret: Egyptian goddess of music

Minerva: Roman goddess of art and crafts

Nataraja (an Incarnation of Shiva): Hindu god of art and dance

Odin: Norse god of poetry and inspiration

Pan: Greek god of dance and flute music

Ptah: Egyptian god of creativity, sculptors, and crafts

Quetzalcoatl: Aztec god of arts and crafts

Saraswati: Hindu goddess of arts, music, writing, and creativity

Seshat: Egyptian goddess of written words, books, and measurements

Thoth: Egyptian god of writing, records, and the patron god of libraries

Vulcan: Roman god of the forge and metalsmithing

Bibliography

Adisa, Opal Palmer. *Eros Muse: Poems and Essays.* Trenton, NJ: Africa World Press, 2006.

Aromatech. "Aromas to Get into the Right Artistic Mood." August 16, 2019. https://aromatechscent.com/blogs /scenting/aromatherapy-to-get-into-the-right-artistic-mood. (Page defunct.)

Athanassakis, Apostolos N., trans. *Hesiod: Theogony, Works and Days, Shield.* 2nd ed. Baltimore, MA: Johns Hopkins University Press, 2004.

Babcock, Jay. "Magic Is Afoot: A Conversation with Alan Moore About the Arts and the Occult." *Arthur,* May 2003. https://arthurmag.com/2007/05/10/1815/.

Basile, Lisa Marie. *City Witchery: Accessible Rituals, Practices & Prompts for Conjuring and Creating in a Magical Metropolis.* Bellevue, WA: Quarto, 2021.

———. *Magical Writing Grimoire: Use the Word as Your Wand for Magic, Manifestation & Ritual.* Beverly, MA: Fair Winds Press, 2020.

Beaumont, John. *An Historical, Psychological, and Theological Treatise of Spirits, Apparitions, Witchcrafts, and Other Magical Practices.* London: D. Browne, 1705.

Betz, Hans Dieter, ed. *The Greek Magical Papyri in Translation.* Chicago: University of Chicago Press, 1986.

Brenner, Grant Hilary. "Your Brain on Creativity." *Psychology Today,* February 22, 2018. https://www.psychologytoday .com/us/blog/experimentations/201802/your-brain-creativity.

Burkert, Walter. *Greek Religion.* Translated by John Raffan. Cambridge, MA: Harvard University Press, 1985.

Cameron, Julia, and Mark Bryan. *The Artist's Way: A Spiritual Path to Higher Creativity.* New York: Putnam, 1992.

Cézanne, Paul. *The Dream of the Poet, or The Kiss of the Muse.* 1860. Oil on canvas. Musée d'Orsay, Paris.

Clear, James. *Atomic Habits: An Easy and Proven Way to Build Good Habits & Break Bad Ones.* New York: Avery, 2018.

Cleary, Thomas, and Sartaz Aziz. *Twilight Goddess: Spiritual Feminism and Feminine Spirituality.* London: Shambala, 2000.

"The Codex Gigas." Kungl Biblioteket. Accessed June 18, 2022. https://www.kb.se/in-english/the-codex-gigas.html.

Cowan, Tom. *Fire in the Head: Shamanism and the Celtic Spirit.* New York: HarperCollins, 1993.

Diaz, Juliet. *Plant Witchery: Discover the Sacred Language, Wisdom, and Magic of 200 Plants.* Carlsbad, CA: Hay House, 2020.

Donaldson-Evans, Catherine. "An Interview with Sci-Fi Legend Ray Bradbury." Fox News. Last modified May 20, 2015. https://www.foxnews.com/story/an-interview-with-sci-fi -legend-ray-bradbury.

Doyle, Charles Clay, Wolfgang Meider, and Fred R. Shapiro. *The Dictionary of Modern Proverbs*. New Haven, CT: Yale University Press, 2012.

Dweck, Carol S. *Mindset: The New Psychology for Success*. New York: Random House, 2006.

Elizabeth, S. *The Art of the Occult: A Visual Sourcebook for the Modern Mystic*. London: White Lion Publishing, 2020.

Estés, Clarissa Pinkola. *Women Who Run With the Wolves: Myths and Stories and the Wild Woman Archetype*. New York: Ballantine Books, 1995.

Gilbert, Elizabeth. *Big Magic: Creative Living Beyond Fear*. New York: Riverhead Books, 2015.

———. "Your Elusive Creative Genius." Filmed February 2009 at TED2009. TED video, 19:15, transcript. https://www.ted .com/talks/elizabeth_gilbert_your_elusive_creative_genius /transcript.

Gladwell, Malcolm. *Outliers: The Story of Success*. New York: Back Bay Books, 2011.

Grace, Marlee. *How to Not Always Be Working: A Toolkit for Creativity and Radical Self-Care*. New York: HarperCollins Publishers, 2018.

Greene, Robert. *Mastery*. London: Penguin Books, 2012.

Grimassi, Raven. *The Witch's Familiar: Spiritual Partners for Successful Magic*. St. Paul, MN: Llewellyn Publications, 2003.

Grohl, Dave. *The Storyteller: Tales of Life and Music*. New York: William Morrow, 2021.

Grossman, Pam. *Waking the Witch: Reflections on Women, Magic, and Power*. New York: Simon and Schuster, 2019.

Heller, Cathy. *Don't Keep Your Day Job: How to Turn Your Passion into Your Career.* New York: St. Martin's Press, 2019.

Herkes, Michael. *Witchcraft for Daily Self-Care: Nourishing Rituals & Spells for a More Balanced Life.* Emeryville, CA: Rockridge Press, 2021.

Hesiod. *Poetry of Theogony.* In *Brill's Companion to Hesiod.* Edited by Antonios Rengakos, Christos Tsagalis, and Franco Montanari. Leiden, Netherlands: Brill, 2009.

"History of the Codex Gigas." Kungl Biblioteket. Accessed June 18, 2022. https://www.kb.se/in-english/the-codex-gigas /history-of-the-codex-gigas.html.

Hofmann, Hans. *Search for the Real.* Edited by Sarah T. Weeks and Bartlett H. Hayes Jr. Rev. ed. Cambridge, MA: MIT Press, 1967.

Houser, Steve. "Seeds for the Future: How to Plant an Acorn." Arborilogical. March 26, 2016. https://www.arborilogical .com/articles/all-articles/article-repository/2013/march /seeds-for-the-future-how-to-plant-an-acorn/.

"How to Say 'Yes, And.'" Second City. Accessed February 26, 2022. https://www.secondcity.com/how-to-say-yes-and.

Hunter, Devin. "S9E19: Casting Spells with Jason Mankey." *Modern Witch.* March 25, 2022. MP3 audio, 60:24. https:// podcasts.apple.com/us/podcast/s9e19-casting-spells -with-jason-mankey/id365213280?i=1000555262769.

———. *The Witch's Book of Mysteries.* Woodbury, MN: Llewellyn Publications, 2019.

———. *The Witch's Book of Spirits.* Woodbury, MN: Llewellyn Publications, 2017.

Hyde, Lewis. *Common as Air: Revolution, Art, and Ownership.* New York: Farrar, Straus, and Giroux, 2010.

———. *The Gift: How the Creative Spirit Transforms the World.* 3rd ed. New York: Vintage Books, 2019.

"An Interview with Alicia Ostriker." *Nashville Review.* August 1, 2012. https://as.vanderbilt.edu/nashvillereview /archives/5452.

Kelden. "The Magic of Persephone: An Interview with Wendy Rule." *By Athame and Stang* (blog). Patheos. July 9, 2019. https://www.patheos.com/blogs/byathameandstang/2019/07 /persephone-wendy-rule/.

King, Steven. "The Writing Life." *Washington Post*, October 1, 2006. https://www.washingtonpost.com/wp-dyn/content /article/2006/09/28/AR2006092801398_pf.html.

Korb, Alex. "Predictable Fear: Why the Brain Likes Haunted Houses." *Psychology Today*, October 31, 2014. https://www .psychologytoday.com/us/blog/prefrontal-nudity/201410 /predictable-fear.

Kynes, Sandra. *Llewellyn's Complete Book of Correspondences.* Woodbury, MN: Llewellyn Publications, 2017.

Laing, Gordon Jennings. *Survivals of Roman Religion.* New York: Cooper Square Publishers, 1963.

Lamott, Anne. *Bird by Bird: Some Instructions on Writing and Life.* New York: Bantam Doubleday Dell Publishing Group, 1980.

Lorca, Federico García. *In Search of Duende.* 2nd ed. New York: New Directions, 1998.

———. "Theory and Play of the Duende." Translated by A. S. Kline. Poetry in Translation, 2007. https://www.poetryin translation.com/PITBR/Spanish/LorcaDuende.php.

Maignan, Albert. *Green Muse*. 1895. Musée de Picardie, Amiens.

Malchiodi, Cathy A. *Art Therapy Sourcebook*. Los Angeles: Lowell House, 1998.

Mankey, Jason, and Astrea Taylor. *Modern Witchcraft with the Greek Gods*. Woodbury, MN: Llewellyn Publications, 2022.

Mankey, Jason. *The Horned God of the Witches*. Woodbury, MN: Llewellyn Publications, 2021.

"The Many Famous Artists Inspired by Absinthe." Absinthia. May 11, 2022. https://absinthia.com/blogs/absinthias-blog /the-many-famous-artists-who-have-been-inspired-by -absinthe.

Monet, Claude. *Water Lilies*. 1903. Musée Marmottan Monet, Paris.

Mueller, Mickie. "The Magical Art of the Well Worn Path." Lewellyn. January 30, 2006. https://www.llewellyn.com /journal/article/1047.

Nagoski, Emily, and Amelia Nagoski. *Burnout: The Secret to Unlocking the Stress Cycle*. New York: Ballantine Books, 2019.

Nagy, Gregory. "Hesiod and the Ancient Biographical Traditions." Harvard Center for Hellenic Studies. November 2, 2020. https://chs.harvard.edu/curated-article/gregory -nagy-hesiod-and-the-ancient-biographical-traditions/.

Newnes, George, ed. "Pictures in Music." *The Strand Magazine*. Vol. 35. January–June 1908. https://archive.org/stream /in.ernet.dli.2015.24894/2015.24894.The-Strand-Magazine -1908-Vol35_djvu.txt.

Newport, Cal. *Deep Work: Rules for Focused Success in a Distracted World.* New York: Grand Central Publishing, 2016.

Oakes, Brian, dir. *ReMastered: Devil at the Crossroads: A Robert Johnson Story.* Scotts Valley, CA: Netflix Originals, 2019.

Orwell, George. *Why I Write.* New York: Penguin Group, 2005.

Parker, Fred. *The Devil as Muse: Blake, Byron, and the Adversary.* Waco, TX: Baylor University Press, 2011.

Parker, Nils. "The Angel in the Marble: Modern Life Lessons from History's Greatest Sculptor." Medium. July 9, 2013. https://nilsaparker.medium.com/the-angel-in-the-marble -f7aa43f333dc.

Patterson, Daniel. "Shaker Gift Paintings." Folkstreams. January 18, 2022. https://www.folkstreams.net/contexts /shaker-gift-paintings.

Pearson, Nicholas. *Crystal Basics: The Energetic, Healing, & Spiritual Power of 200 Gemstones.* Rochester, VT: Destiny Books, 2020.

Plato. *Essential Dialogues of Plato.* Translated by Benjamin Jowett. New York: Barnes & Noble Classics, 2005.

Pressfield, Steven. *The War of Art: Break Through the Blocks and Win Your Creative Battles.* New York: Black Irish Entertainment, 2012.

Roberts, Molly. *Art Magick: How to Become an Art Witch and Unlock Your Creative Power.* Exeter, UK: David and Charles, 2022.

Rousseau, Henri. *The Muse Inspiring the Poet.* 1909. Oil on canvas. Kunstsammlung Basel, Basel.

Sappho. *Sappho.* Translated by Mary Barnard. Berkeley: University of California Press, 1958.

Shaffer, Pam. "Ep 95: Tori Amos." October 27, 2021, in *Why Not Both*. Produced by Laura Studarus and *Under the Radar* magazine, podcast, MP3 audio, 60:08, https://anchor.fm /why-not-both/episodes/Ep-95-Tori-Amos-e198uoj.

Stavish, Mark. *Egregores: The Occult Entities That Watch over Human Destiny*. Rochester, VT: Inner Traditions, 2018.

Stein, Diane. *Stroking the Python: Women's Psychic Lives*. St. Paul, MN: Llewellyn Publications, 1988.

Summers, Montague, trans. *The Malleus Maleficarum of Heinrich Kramer and James Sprenger*. New York: Dover, 1971.

Three Initiates. *The Kybalion: A Study of the Hermetic Philosophy of Ancient Egypt and Greece*. Chicago: The Yogi Publication Society, 1908.

Veilwalker, Obsidian. "Magickal Properties and Correspondences of Tea and Coffee." Plentiful Earth. June 16, 2021. https://plentifulearth.com/magickal-properties-and -correspondences-of-tea-and-coffee/.

Vylenz, DeZ. *The Mindscape of Alan Moore*. London: Shadowsnake Films, 2008.

Weigle, Martha. *Spiders & Spinsters: Women and Mythology*. Albuquerque: University of New Mexico Press, 1982.

Weinstein, Edie. "The Marilyn Monroe Effect: The Nonverbal Communication of Confidence." Psych Central. Last modified September 2, 2019. https://psychcentral.com/blog/the -marilyn-monroe-effect-the-nonverbal-communication -of-confidence.

Whitehurst, Tess. "Do the Magic, Then Do the Work." In *Llewellyn's 2021 Witches' Companion: A Guide to Contemporary*

Living, 223–30. Woodbury, MN: Llewellyn Publications, 2020.

Windling, Terri. "On the Care and Feeding of Daemons and Muses." *Myth & Moore* (blog), October 13, 2015. https:// www.terriwindling.com/blog/2015/10/the-muse.html.

Yeats, W. B. *Fairy and Folk Tales of the Irish Peasantry.* London: Walter Scott, 1888.

Zafarris, Jess. "Did Hemingway Say 'Write Drunk, Edit Sober'? Nope—He Preferred to Write Sober." Writer's Digest. December 20, 2018. https://www.writersdigest.com/be -inspired/did-hemingway-say-write-drunk-edit-sober -nope-he-preferred-to-write-sober.

Zakroff, Laura Tempest. Keynote Ritual. Pagan Fires. Clarks-ville, OH, 2019.

———. *Sigil Witchery: A Witch's Guide to Crafting Magick Symbols.* Woodbury, MN: Llewellyn Publications, 2018.

Zap, Jonathan. "The Path of the Numinous: Living and Work-ing with the Creative Muse." Zap Oracle. March 19, 2014. https://zaporacle.com/the-path-of-the-numinous-living -and-working-with-the-creative-muse/.

Zomorodi, Manoush. *Bored and Brilliant: How Spacing Out Can Unlock Your Most Productive & Creative Self.* New York: St. Martin's Press, 2017.

To Write to the Author

If you wish to contact the author or would like more information about this book, please write to the author in care of Llewellyn Worldwide Ltd. and we will forward your request. Both the author and the publisher appreciate hearing from you and learning of your enjoyment of this book and how it has helped you. Llewellyn Worldwide Ltd. cannot guarantee that every letter written to the author can be answered, but all will be forwarded. Please write to:

Astrea Taylor
% Llewellyn Worldwide
2143 Wooddale Drive
Woodbury, MN 55125-2989

Please enclose a self-addressed stamped envelope for reply,
or $1.00 to cover costs. If outside the U.S.A., enclose
an international postal reply coupon.

Many of Llewellyn's authors have websites with additional information and resources. For more information, please visit our website at http://www.llewellyn.com.